If you need large print in order to read, you may qualify for Wolfner Library services that include free access by mail or internet to:

- Over 280,000 books in audio, braille, and large print
- Over 70 audio magazines and 500 audio newspapers
- Use of digital player for audio books and magazines
- Free app for online access to audio books, magazines, and braille files

Wolfner Talking Book and Braille Library

Email: Wolfner@sos.mo.gov
Toll free: (800) 392-2614
Phone: (573) 751-8720
www.sos.mo.gov/wolfner

The Red Hat Society's Laugh Lines

Also by Sue Ellen Cooper
The Red Hat Society®

The Red Hat Society's Laugh Lines

Stories of Inspiration and Hattitude

Sue Ellen Cooper

Illustrations by Andrea Reekstin

DOUBLEDAY LARGE PRINT HOME LIBRARY EDITION

WARNER BOOKS

NEW YORK   BOSTON

This Large Print Edition, prepared especially for Doubleday Large Print Home Library, contains the complete, unabridged text of the original Publisher's Edition.

Warner Books

Time Warner Book Group
1271 Avenue of the Americas, New York, NY 10020

Printed in the United States of America
First Edition: April 2005

ISBN 0-7394-5413-7

Cover design by Brigid Pearson
Cover photo by Herman Estevez

This Large Print Book carries the
Seal of Approval of N.A.V.H.

To Allen, Andrea, Matt, Sabrina, and Debra for your hard work and unfailing dedication to the mission of the Red Hat Society and its members. You are worth your weight in rubies!

Acknowledgments

Many thanks to Jenny Bent and Amy Einhorn for their hard work and support, and to my little dog, Frosty, for lying patiently at my feet for the countless hours it took to write this book.

Contents

A Note from Sue Ellen

Five years ago, I had a "happy accident." I gave my friend a copy of a famous poem and a red hat—and by doing so, I inadvertently started a women's movement. As I write this, nearly five years later, the Red Hat Society has over 35,000 chapters—over 35,000!—and continues to grow at an astonishing pace. I still find all of this very hard to believe.

I wrote our first book, *The Red Hat Society: Fun and Friendship After Fifty,* in order to share the warmth, camaraderie, and sisterhood that we Red Hatters enjoy not only with our Red Hat Society sisters but also with other women (no matter their age) of kindred spirit. Our members were sharing stories with us—stories that were far too good to keep to ourselves—of how the Red Hat Society grew and developed, and the meaningful place it was assuming in their lives.

Since the publication of our first book, more wonderful stories from Red Hatters have continued to pour in via E-mail, letters, and phone calls. We are beginning to see ourselves as members of one big family, developing strong bonds of trust and caring. Because of this, we feel free to share our real selves and our real-life experiences with our newfound sisters. This kind of sharing is downright good for our spirits and our souls!

We are many things to many people—mothers, grandmothers, daughters, and wives. We seek and enjoy new experiences; we travel; we create; we have adventures. So it is natural that we share stories concerning *all* of these things with others with whom we feel connected. As we love to say, "We are not *done* yet!" Since we are not done, the stories keep coming. Thus, this second book.

The seasons of life leave their marks on our faces: We like to call them "laugh lines" (and sometimes "cry lines"). And we try to be proud of them. After all, we don't want to look like twenty-two-year-old models.

(Okay, sometimes we do, especially when we're trying on bathing suits.) But we are comfortable in our skin, wrinkled though it may be, because life has bestowed upon us the consolation prizes of wisdom and gratitude. Wisdom has come as result of all that has befallen us; gratitude is what we feel for the rich relationships and experiences we have had so far, as well as for the additional gift of the time ahead, time in which to continue to grow and learn. (And, inevitably, add even more lines to our faces!)

When a woman joins the Red Hat Society and lowers that red hat onto her head, magic seems to ensue. New friendships are born; old friendships are solidified or rediscovered. But what this new book, which you now hold in your hands, will demonstrate is that this magic is not limited to the times when we are actually *wearing* those red hats. In fact, some of the most amazing things happen to us when we leave our hats at home! As much as we may think it's wearing a red hat that emboldens us, that makes the world sit up and take notice of us, we discover that the hat is only a symbol of something deeper.

We members of the Red Hat Society are

each a part of something important. We belong. We matter. We count among our members a fifty-two-year-old Olympian who will compete in her sixth Olympics in 2006, world travelers who show no signs of slowing down, artists, writers, and other creative, vital women from all walks of life. We are all sisters and each one of us brings something to the party. We never know when and where we will run into another of these wonderful women, as we continue to find one another in the most unlikely of places (like a bathroom in the Caribbean!). Stories of such experiences and connections will touch your heart and make you proud to belong to our sisterhood (whether you're a Red Hatter officially or just in spirit).

The world is a confusing place. On the one hand, there is tremendous suffering, grief, and strife, and on the other, there is still so much joy and beauty in such things as a grandchild's smile or a friend's voice on the phone at just the right time. We owe it to one another to share the good times—and the bad. When we do, we learn that we are not alone. We have an entire sisterhood—women who sometimes wear red and purple—to share with.

I hope you enjoy these new stories. At the end of the book, you will find some blank pages where you may wish to record some of your own stories, and I hope you will encourage your red-hatted sisters to share theirs, as well. Remember your mother teaching you how important it is to share? She was probably talking about possessions then, but surely she knew that sharing in any way is life-enhancing. As we all realize now, mothers know best.

—Sue Ellen Cooper, October 11, 2004

Introduction

The Incomparable Value
of Laughter

**Laughter is the sun that drives
winter from the human race.**
—Victor Hugo

Laughing deeply is living deeply.
—Milan Kundera

**Wrinkles should merely indicate
where smiles have been.**
—Mark Twain

We members of the Red Hat Society don
our red hats and purple dresses at the age
of fifty. Half a century of living will put lines
on any face—hence the "laugh lines" referred to in the title of this book. Anyone
who is adverse to deepening her laugh lines
may wish to avoid membership in the Red
Hat Society as well, because this is what we

are all about. But faces will also reflect tears shed. Life shows on our countenances, doesn't it?

 "Remember, we get better-looking wrinkles from laughing than from frowning."
—*Ruth Walker (Order of the Crimson Sage, Wallace, North Carolina)*

Bonding usually occurs automatically among women who regularly spend time together. What makes the Red Hat Society special is that we go beyond merely spending time together. We devote time to coming up with activities that are guaranteed to be fun. And fun activities inevitably lead to that venerable line inducer—laughter!

Imagine you are a set director in the theater. After reading a play to be presented and soaking up its mood, you are charged with creating an appropriate stage environment for it. If a play is serious, perhaps sad or thought-provoking in tone, the backdrop will probably be heavy and dark. All the stage props will be carefully chosen to reflect the theme, as well. These choices will subtly set the mood for the audience, even before the first line of dialogue is spoken. All that heaviness will not be lost on them.

If the play is a comedy, the colors used to paint the set will be cheerful and lively. The lighting will be bright. The props will be whimsical. From the time the members of the audience file into the theater, they will be primed to set aside their troubles and concerns for a while and prepare to enjoy themselves.

"Shared laughter is like throwing open the shutters in a gloomy room and letting in fresh air and sunshine."
—*Lila Green*

When we Red Hat Society chapterettes plan our get-togethers, we are deliberately setting the stage for fun. When each member takes her turn planning a gathering, she has full latitude to dream up an activity that appeals to her, knowing that her circle of pals is going to be game to join her in that adventure. Not only is she encouraged to let her playful child venture out into the sunshine: She is assured of playmates!

When you get an invitation to your next chapter event (via phone call, E-mail, or snail mail), it is likely that you will immediately begin to feel anticipation. When you find out that Donna has planned for the group to play miniature golf (in full regalia) and then go for ice-cream sundaes, you will begin to look forward to having a lot of fun with your playmates. A week or a month later, when Karen plans a field trip to that art museum (the one you have never had time to visit), you will begin to look forward to getting to see it at long last. When Susan surprises you with a 6:00 A.M. phone call and bids you to a come-as-you-are party, you will have to smile (even as you wince!). You have had a glimpse of the stage set— and you can begin to make mental preparations to enjoy yourself. You have just received a permission slip for your next play date!

I believe this is the true strength of the Red Hat Society. Together, we are learning to plan adventures deliberately, to encourage one another to find humor wherever it is to be found, and to wring every last morsel

of joy out of life. We know that there is nothing better than the sense of freedom and
happiness that results from playing together. Playing or hanging out, goofing off,
recess—whatever we decide to call it—lifts
the weight of years, the burdens of the soul.
This playing leads to what is indeed one of
life's greatest gifts: laughter!

 "Every time a man smiles, and
much more when he laughs, it adds
something to his fragment of life."
—*Laurence Sterne*

Laughter is good—and good *for* you, too.
All of us know that from personal experience. We have all known the wonderful "all
is well with the world" sensation that per-
vades our inner beings while we enjoy a
deep belly laugh. Remember the wonderful
movies of the sixties (*The Pink Panther, A
Shot in the Dark*) featuring Peter Sellers as
Inspector Clouseau? I remember being in a
theater, with several hundred other movie-
goers, all of us positively screaming with
laughter. In that sort of situation, laughter is
contagious. I recall feeling deep gratitude to
the filmmakers for giving me such a gift.

And there is something about being in the presence of others, even strangers, who are helpless with glee that prompts us to laugh, too. Often it takes only one hearty laugher to spur others to join in. So even laughter among strangers is communicable.

It is impossible to laugh without finding yourself momentarily immersed in joy. And when we find something extremely funny, the pleasure is greatly amplified if we can turn to someone we love, share it with them, and watch them laugh, too. Their enjoyment is communicated to us and we get caught up in the fun all over again. In that warm moment of shared experience, we draw closer to one another.

I have heard that children laugh around four hundred times a day. Adults, in sharp contrast, laugh only ten to fifteen times or so—and even those expressions of humor are apt to be subdued smiles or snickers, not belly laughs. Is this because we adults have lost our ability to be spontaneous, or are we just too sophisticated to allow ourselves to express, or even experience unfettered delight easily? Maybe both.

What is more contagious than the bubbling belly laugh of a small child? Not long ago, there was a sound bite being passed around the Internet: It consisted of nothing more than a recording of a baby laughing out loud. Talk about delightful! No matter how many times we played that at Hatquarters, we laughed yet again.

 "Laughter is like the human body wagging its tail."
—*Anne Wilson Schaef*

When we get together with old friends, sharing reminiscences of funny situations can cause us to erupt in laughter at them all over again (even if they weren't all that funny at the time). We have probably all had the experience of being with people who are laughing about some shared experience from their mutual past, one in which we did not share. I think the saying "You had to be there" is true; we probably found those stories only mildly amusing. Why? Because you *did* have to be there.

Sharing potentially humorous moments with someone close to you can be dangerous, too. Something that might bring a fleeting smile (or perhaps a guilty snicker) when you are alone can explode into sidesplitting guffaws, perhaps at inappropriate times, if you're in the company of another.

When my husband, Allen, and I were young college students, we attended a chamber-music concert in order to satisfy a requirement of a music class I was taking. I remember the audience growing respectfully quiet as the tastefully black-clad musicians filed onto the stage, seated themselves, and, with great gravity, began to play a slow, somber piece.

I can't recall what originally made me want to giggle. It could have been a nervous reaction to an unfamiliar experience, maybe a stray, discordant note hit by one of the oh-so-serious musicians, or just my immaturity and inability to "settle down and behave," which my stern inner parent was ordering me to do. (Occasionally, my inner child can misbehave. How about yours?) Whatever caused it, I could feel a bubble of suppressed laughter rising in my throat, and I knew that I must avoid meeting Allen's eyes, because I could sense his body, next to mine, tensing, too. Inevitably, we glanced sideways at each other. Each of us caught the answering glint of amusement in the other's eyes, and we both began, with a rising sense of embarrassed horror, to giggle. The harder we tried to stop, the harder we laughed, and tears began to stream from our eyes. In the interest of good manners (and to avoid stoning by the audience), we slunk from the auditorium. But, of course, the minute we got outside, we burst out laughing again. Was anything really all that funny? I'm sure it wasn't—not to anyone else anyway. But that really didn't matter. It was just one of those times of shared hilarity, which, thirty-seven years later, we still recall with amusement.

"Against the assault of laughter, nothing can stand."
—*Mark Twain*

Interestingly enough, no one can make you laugh against your will. Have you ever laughed your head off at a movie or a book and then recommended it to someone else, someone who later told you they just didn't "get it"? How disappointing that can be. In a sense, it can make you feel lonely for a moment. Unsuccessfully trying to share humor carries a small sense of loss—the loss of a potential spontaneous connection of spirits. But this just reinforces the point: Sharing humor *is* precious.

 "We cannot really love anybody with whom we never laugh."
—*Agnes Ripplier*

 "Laughter is the closest thing to the grace of God."
—*Karl Barth*

Okay, we can all agree that laughter is excellent for our moods. But it is truly amazing to discover the beneficial effects laughter has on our physical beings. If it were possible to bottle laughter and sell it as a medicine, it would be too expensive for any of us to afford. Thank goodness it's free!

At the 2004 Red Hat Society's annual convention in Dallas, we were fortunate to be regaled with the antics and advice of a self-proclaimed "laughter therapist," "Dr. Maxine Harper." Maxine's alter ego, Joanne Sabol-Augenstein, has since become a valued friend of mine, as well as the "Queen of Mirth and Merriment" of her own Red Hat Society chapter. Having made an in-depth study of the benefits of laughter on the body, she has shared some of her findings with me. If anybody thinks for one moment that Red Hatting and the laughter it naturally brings with it has no *real* value, I invite the doubter to read on.

- Laughter can strengthen your immune system. The value of a strong immune system cannot be overemphasized, as it helps fight off infection, allergic conditions, and, research suggests, even some forms of cancer.
- When the coin is flipped, we discover that negative emotions, such as anxiety, depression, and suppressed anger, can weaken the immune system, diminishing our ability to fight off infections and other serious illnesses.
- Laughter has been proven to increase the level of antibodies in our systems and lower the incidence of "killer lymphocytes" (a type of white blood cell). Researchers have found more antibodies present in the mucus of the nose and respiratory passages of those who have recently enjoyed a good laugh. It seems more than possible that frequent laughter

could be a factor in reducing the incidence of colds, sore throats, and bronchial infections.

- Laughter is a natural painkiller. It can increase the body's level of endorphins (natural pain relievers), possibly preventing pain's onset and definitely reducing the intensity of pain already present in the body. It has been shown to lessen the perceived pain of arthritis, muscle spasms, and even tension headaches. My friend Joanne quotes one migraine sufferer as saying laughter doesn't banish her headaches entirely, but it greatly diminishes them for a time and reduces their intensity significantly.

 "It has always seemed to me that hearty laughter is a good way to jog internally without having to go outdoors."
—*Norman Cousins*

Sixteen years ago, I had an interesting personal experience with laughter following abdominal surgery. The day I came home from the hospital, my friends Carol and

John Sibley stopped by for a brief visit and dropped off a couple of videos they had rented for me. They knew I was going to be lolling on the sofa for a day or two and so thoughtfully supplied some entertainment. That evening, I popped one of the movies into the VCR and settled back into the sofa pillows for a little R and R. The movie, *Planes, Trains, & Automobiles,* starring Steve Martin and John Candy, was hilarious. I found myself laughing uncontrollably while simultaneously pressing on my recent incision. It was getting a painful workout! I had heard of laughing so hard it hurts, but I had never experienced it to quite that degree before. Of course, I could have shut off the movie at any time, but the pleasure of the laughter—a healing elixir of great power—was so intense that it was worth the sharp physical pain it caused!

 "Laughter is a gift everyone should open."
—*Gene Mitchener*

Joanne mentioned two additional health benefits provided by laughter:

- A smile cools down the blood to the hypothalamus gland (who knows how?) and a frown heats it up. Can we all agree that it is always better to be cool?
- The muscles we use in smiling have been shown to send signals to the brain, causing it to send beneficial and pleasurable hormones flooding through the body. Apparently, the brain doesn't differentiate between forced smiles and laughs and genuine ones. All that smiling and laughing is accepted, literally, at face value. So the beneficial hormones get released whether or not the outward expressions of mirth are genuine. I guess the brain says to itself, We seem to be having a lot of fun here! Better release some of those hormones.

Do you remember the Disney movie *Pollyanna*? Hayley Mills played an orphaned child who was sent to live with her sour aunt whose name was Polly. Although the little girl, Pollyanna, had had some hard knocks in her life, she seemed to see only the best in every person and situation she encountered. Her effervescent personality and unquenchable optimism spread joy throughout their small town, eventually winning over even the staid Aunt Polly.

The character of Pollyanna was so relentlessly upbeat that her very name has come to be used by cynics to define a person who is blindly, even foolishly, optimistic. But if the preceding information is true, it follows that a Pollyanna is going to have a very healthy body—*and* psyche.

 "We don't laugh because we're happy—we're happy because we laugh."
—*William James*

 "Humor has great power to heal on an emotional level. You can't hold anger, you can't hold fear, you can't hold hurt while you're laughing."
—*Steve Bhaerman*

If this is true, it follows that cultivating the habit of curving the lips up at the corners and squeezing out a giggle or two at not much of anything can actually be very good for you. Try it; you'll like it!

"Get out of bed forcing a smile. You may not smile because you are cheerful: but if you will force yourself to smile you'll . . . be cheerful because you smile."
—*Kenneth Goode*

A word about cry lines is in order here, as well. There will be no avoiding these. Just like the proverbial death and taxes, they are inevitable, and they will show on our faces, too. Even a Pollyanna will not be able to laugh in the face of serious illness or loss. But when we cry, our friends can help. Though our suffering may cause us to be poor company, true friends will be there to offer what they can—perhaps a soft smile of remembrance or the tight embrace of a loving hug. In cases like these, we know that it is not helpful to try to force humor or make inane comments about "looking on the bright side." But patience and empathy are similar in character to humor, and we *can* offer those.

"Peace begins with a smile."
—*Mother Teresa*

Continuing to cultivate one's capacity for optimism is valuable and adds much to our lives, and, by extension, to the lives of those around us. If we allow too much anger, worry, and fear into our lives, these negative emotions will render us useless (and unappealing) to others.

I once had a seemingly insignificant experience that had a large impact on my life. I was driving home, fuming over an extremely negative encounter I had just had with a highly disagreeable person, almost looking for someone to take my out my anger on. Suddenly, a car shot out of a driveway in front of me, causing me to hit the brakes hard. In a ripple effect, this caused a pile of carefully organized stuff to slide from my backseat into a heap on the floor, escalating my bad mood considerably. The same car veered back into my lane as we both tried to enter the freeway and continued to swerve erratically. Angrily, I sped up and passed the female driver, turning to give her a glower in the process. But when I glimpsed her face, my "righteous" anger evaporated, and shame and pity took its place. She was sobbing uncontrollably, her face contorted in pain. I remembered that the place she had first cut me off was the exit from the hospital. God only knew what kind of experience she might have just come from. As I cast a silent prayer for her heavenward, I also asked for more grace and empathy in my own life.

" . . . we need to let go of some of our problems and worries and remember what it was like to be kids . . . to play if we choose to and laugh through our tears if we have to. We women have long been the backbone of our country as well as of our families and we must continue to show the strength our foremothers did. We must hold out our hands as well as our hearts, as some of us will have many tears yet to shed in our lives. . . . The Red Hatters stand for living and giving strength to those who need a new friend, solace to those who may be in need, and friendship to those who desire it. We are the women of the Red Hat Society."

—*Diana Stanchic (Pittsburgh Red Hat Mamas, Pennsylvania)*

I have learned that staying on the lookout for opportunities to smile and laugh is paramount. This habit makes us healthier and happier people. Healthy and happy people make the world a better place for others as well as for ourselves.

As far as I'm concerned, Pollyanna had it right.

1

L.O.L. (Laughing Out Loud)—at Ourselves

Growing old is mandatory. Growing up is optional.

—Author unknown

There's not one shred of evidence supporting the notion that life is serious.

—Author unknown

We Red Hatters take our silliness seriously. We believe that the deliberate cultivation of a healthy sense of humor can transform many a life situation, and, really, there are so many funny things to smile at or laugh *about* if you stay alert and watch for them. Lighthearted playfulness is our way of amusing ourselves and one another, and my, can it be effective! This spirit is evident in our chapter names, our titles, our outfits, and in every activity we plan. Whether you're a giggler, a chortler, a chuckler, a hand-over-the-mouth titterer, a guffawer, or (God forbid) a snorter, you are warned to avoid consuming liquids while reading this chapter. (It's only funny when milk comes out of someone else's nose.)

For those of you who are new to the Red Hat Society, I'd like to introduce you to Ruby. Ruby is our official mascot, and she epitomizes this ability to laugh better than anyone I know. For those of you who are old friends with Ruby, I'm pleased to say that she'll be accompanying you throughout this book.

THE FUNNY PAGES

 "You're never too old to do goofy stuff."
—*Ward Cleaver*

It has been said, "Blessed is he who can laugh at himself, for he shall never cease to be amused." How true that is! The quickest and easiest place to look for a source of humor is within ourselves. Fortunately, we Red Hatters are capable of enjoying a good laugh at our own expense! And in addition to that, we are secure enough to share those stories with others, knowing that they will get as big a kick out of them as we do.

Susan Powers (the Fabulous Founders, Fullerton, California) needs reading glasses, as does her husband, Bob. "He would frequently lose his glasses," she says, "and ask me to help find them. This went on for months. Finally, one night while I was contentedly reading, he came into the room and asked if I had seen his glasses. I was so exasperated that I flipped out, telling him I was not the keeper of his glasses and that he needed to keep track of them himself. In the midst of my barrage, I realized that he was looking at me with a very strange expression on his face. I stopped long enough to ask him why he was looking at me that way. You can imagine my embarrassment when he said, 'You're wearing my glasses.' "

Is there really such a thing as coincidence? Some of us don't think so. If you've lived long enough, you've probably had a lot of encounters with what feels like divine Providence. Gay Mentes (Red Hot Jazzy Ladies, Kelowna, British Columbia, Canada) writes: "Way back over a quarter of a century ago, when I was about a quarter of a century old, I was living in Lumby and decided to make the move to Vancouver, a few hours west. Before I left, some people I knew mentioned that their son was a policeman in Vancouver. The father said, 'If my son ever stops you, tell him I said not to give you a ticket!' Several months passed and I was out and about one evening, when sure enough I was pulled over. I knew I had been going a little quickly, and my life flashed before my eyes. The policeman came over and I handed him my license and registration. 'I see you're from Lumby,' he said. 'My folks live in Lumby.' The wheels in my head started turning. Could it be possible? I said, 'Are your parents Willie and Mike Porter?' And he said, 'Yes!' I wondered if I dared, and I replied, 'Your dad told me before I left that if you ever pulled me over, I should tell you that he says not to give me a ticket!' We chatted for a few minutes, and guess what? He sent me on my way with just a warning!"

We may have to struggle with inconveniences, but we'll never lose our sense of humor! Queen Karen Sizemore (the Ellet Hat Flashers, Akron, Ohio) was experiencing repeated problems with her new hip replacement. It kept popping out of its socket. One day, it happened again, and she called 911 to get someone to take her to the emergency room—again. Since her doors were locked, the emergency team had to go in through a window. As she stood on her good leg, favoring her bad hip, a skinny young fireman tumbled onto her bed from the window. Grinning broadly, he rolled over and said, "Mrs. Sizemore, I'm back in your bed again!" As they took her to the front porch and out to the ambulance, she told her neighbors that she had celebrated her sixty-sixth birthday with five young firemen in her bed. And off she went with her Red Hat Society earrings dangling.

 "I finally got it all together; now I'm falling apart."
—*Anonymous*

Kathy Jeske (the Red Hat Disorder, Santa Clara, California) was passing through security at Kansas City International Airport, piling a big tote bag of books onto the conveyor belt, when her skirt somehow became tangled up with something she was carrying and fell all the way off, puddling around her ankles. (She says she will be forever grateful that she was wearing a slip that day.) With great dignity, she gathered the skirt in her arms and, waiting her turn, passed through the metal detector. Then she scurried behind the machine and hurriedly stepped back into her skirt. There was one highly positive result from this experience: Kathy's companion, who is terrified of flying, laughed so hard at the whole thing that she didn't have time to worry about the takeoff.

Sometimes what gets us is not what we've lost but what we've unknowingly picked up. Judi Simmons (the Ascot Ladies in Red, Sarasota, Florida) went on a vacation to Paris some years ago. Dressed to the nines in high-heeled boots and a long mink coat, she had just left the rest room and was walking through a long lobby. She noticed people looking at her and thought it was due to her fine outfit. She was walking proud when she saw someone pointing. When she turned her head to see what they were looking at, she saw that she was dragging yards of toilet paper behind her!

> "The child in you, like all children, loves to laugh, to be around people who can laugh at themselves and life. Children instinctively know that the more laughter we have in our lives, the better."
> —*Wayne Dyer*

Lynda Herzog-Pope is the queen of Herzog's Hilarious Hellyun Hairdressers and Healthcare Heffers of Haughton in Haughton, Louisiana. (That chapter name *had* to be included in this book.) She tells a tale about herself that would turn our faces as red as our hats if it happened to any of us!

Because she had recently married a man who was a member of the Shriners, Lynda received an invitation to her first formal luncheon for Shriner wives. Her husband urged her to go, telling her that there would be at least a hundred women there and it would give her a chance to start getting acquainted with the wives of his friends. When she arrived, the receptionist could find no record of her reservation, but, overlooking what seemed to be just a slipup, the woman was kind enough to escort Lynda to the last place available, which was at an excellent table right in front. Lynda was glad she had dressed up, as every woman in the room was gorgeously attired. She made small talk with the woman next to her as they enjoyed fabulous appetizers and filet mignon. Then it was time for dessert. The waiters wheeled out a three-tier cake and a second table, this one bearing a pile of beautifully wrapped packages—undoubtedly a stack of door prizes! At this point, a woman with a microphone stepped up to Lynda, saying, "Let's start at this end of the table. Would you introduce yourself and tell everyone your relationship to the bride-to-be?" Lynda stammered that she was so sorry but she had obviously crashed their party! The other women in the room "absolutely screamed with laughter and applause!" It turned out that the Shriners' event was across the hall. But the women insisted that Lynda zip across the hall to put in an appearance and then return to them for dessert, so she did. What friendly people! (Some of them must have been Red Hatters.)

"The happiest people don't necessarily have the best of everything. They just make the best of everything."
—*Anonymous*

Vice Queen Bee Doris D. Meneses from the Red Hat Mamas, Homestead, Florida, is a cantor at an 8:00 A.M. Mass. She sings the music and introduces the hymns to the congregation. One Sunday morning, she was announcing the offertory hymn. She says, "I glanced at the page of the hymnbook and clearly said, 'During the presentation of gifts today, please join me in singing hymn number two seventy-SEX!' I held my breath for a moment and didn't move an inch, hoping that no one else had caught my error. No such luck! Within seconds, there was a tremendous guffaw from the middle of the church and many more parishioners joined in the laughter. I couldn't look at the congregation, so I glanced over at the priest, who was just looking at me with questioning eyes, a large smile on his face. I am not easily embarrassed, but that day I turned all shades of red!" I wonder if she was wearing a purple dress that day; it would have been so serendipitous!

A new version of that not-so-fresh feeling: Princess Daughter Laura McCann (the Red Hat Mamas, Oxford Hills, Norway/Paris, Maine) has two dogs, which she loves dearly. One evening, she heard one of them making ghastly sounds outside. She rushed outdoors and saw that a skunk had bitten him on the cheek and was, in fact, still holding on for dear life. "My dogs are like children to me," says Laura, "so I kicked the skunk with all the strength I could muster. He let go, then turned his back on the three of us. I was scared it was rabid and would attack us, so I took the dogs inside, both of them stinking to high heaven. The vet suggested that douche would be the best way to get the smell out, so I found myself at the grocery store in the middle of the night, smelling terrible, with my arms full of ten boxes of Summer's Eve." Wouldn't we all like to know what was running through that clerk's mind?

Debbie Senseny (the Skyline Red Hats, Wilmington, Delaware) and her ex-husband entered a fishing tournament on Lake Martin in Alexander City, Alabama. "It was at 6:00 A.M. on a Saturday morning, and we were getting ready to put the boat in the lake, when I felt something crawling down my leg. I started screaming and taking off my blue jeans. All the people who had already put their boats in the lake came running to see what was happening." As she lay on the ground in her panties, a good-size crowd gathered around her just in time to see something roll out of her jeans—a cigarette lighter, which had apparently slid through a hole in her jeans pocket.

"Sure I'm for helping the elderly. I'm going to be old myself someday."
—*Lillian Carter (in her eighties at the time)*

Nedra Ellis of the Scarlet O'Hatters in Amarillo, Texas, shared with us what may have been her very first senior moment. During a frustrating shopping trip, Nedra was returning to her dressing room when she saw a woman to her left about to head in her direction. She stopped to let the other woman pass; the other woman waited politely, as well. "We both stood still for several seconds, waiting for someone to make the first move. I decided to continue on my way, but out of the corner of my eye, I saw that she had moved, too. We both jumped back. I was thinking, Lady, if you would just get out of my way, I could get this dressing room ordeal over with. However, what I said aloud was, 'I am so sorry. Please go ahead.' Dead silence. She just stood there. Because, as I realized slowly, that was a mirror and she was my reflection." What do you want to bet Nedra didn't know whether to laugh or to cry?

There's nothing like being totally embarrassed in the comfort of your own home. When Joan Auletta, queen of the Red Hatted Sweet Potatoes in Fort Lauderdale, Florida, lived on Long Island, her whole family was out in the backyard with her husband while she did some cleaning up indoors. Joan was down in the basement, finishing up the last wash of the day, and she pulled off the robe she was wearing (over her birthday suit) and tossed it into the machine. As she hurried upstairs to dress, she saw her son's football helmet on the stairs, waiting to be taken up to his room, so, rather than carry it, she plopped it on her head. As she rounded the newel post on the way to the next flight of stairs, thinking that she was totally alone in the house, she encountered the meter man. He had been let into the house by her husband. The poor guy certainly couldn't have guessed what his wife was (or wasn't) wearing. The meter man stood silently just inside the front door, his mouth hanging open. Says Joan, "I gulped and just walked right by him and up the stairs as if I had never seen him. Can you just imagine him going home and telling his wife about the crazy lady in the basement? My kids are all grown and they still love to tell of Mom's Naked Parade." In my opinion, it takes one brave woman to tell that one about herself!

Joelle Silva, "Design Wizard" of the Crimson Flashes in Antelope, California, tells of an experience she had in the maternity department of a store thirty years ago, when she was there to purchase a nursing bra. Although the tale is not one about herself, she did find it a bit embarrassing and extremely amusing. "In front of me in line," writes Joelle, "there was an adorable old lady who would have been a Red Hatter if we had been around then. She had a nightgown she wanted to purchase, and the clerk said, 'Are you aware that this is a nightgown for nursing mothers?' The lady seemed surprised, and the clerk continued, 'That's why there are these slits in the front under the pleats.' And without batting an eyelash, the little old lady said, 'Oh, I thought those were for papa.' "

DON'T MESS WITH THE LADIES IN RED!

An older lady wearing a beautiful red hat gets pulled over for speeding. . . .

Lady in Red Hat: Is there a problem, Officer?
Officer: Ma'am, you were speeding.
Lady: Oh, I see.
Officer: Can I see your license, please?
Lady: I'd give it to you, but I don't have it.
Officer: You don't have one?

Lady: Lost it four years ago for drunk driving.

Officer: I see. . . . Can I see your vehicle-registration papers, please?

Lady: I can't do that.

Officer: Why not?

Lady: I stole this car.

Officer: Stole it?

Lady: Yes, and I killed and hacked up the owner.

Officer: You what?

Lady: His body parts are in plastic bags, if you want to see.

The officer looks at the woman and slowly backs away to his car and calls for backup. Within minutes, five police cars circle the car. A senior officer slowly approaches the car, clasping his half-drawn gun.

Officer 2: Ma'am, could you step out of your vehicle, please!

The woman steps out of her vehicle.

Lady: Is there a problem, sir?

Officer 2: One of my officers told me that

you have stolen this car and murdered the owner.

Lady: Murdered the owner?

Officer 2: Yes. Could you please open the trunk of your car?

The woman opens the trunk, revealing nothing but an empty trunk.

Officer 2: Is this your car, ma'am?

Lady: Yes, here are the registration papers.

The officer is stunned.

Officer 2: One of my officers claims that you do not have a driver's license.

The woman digs into her handbag and pulls out a clutch purse and hands it to the officer. The officer examines the license. He looks quite puzzled.

Officer 2: Thank you, ma'am. One of my officers told me that you didn't have a license, that you stole this car, and that you murdered and hacked up the owner.

Lady in Red Hat: Bet the liar told you I was speeding, too!

This story was found on the Internet and we changed the "little old lady" to a Red Hatter. This woman *must* have been one of us.

Being a Red Hatter is a special talent, as evidenced by the three-foot-high trophy that stands on the front counter of the Gresham Senior Center in Oregon. The Feisty Red Hatters of Gresham attended a Dairy Daze fund-raiser at the Zimmerman Heritage Farm House. For the talent show, Charlotte Freeman says, the ladies decided to recite and pantomime the Jenny Joseph poem "Warning," complete with spitting on the ground. Despite competition from singing children and a dancing dog, they won! They did mention that they felt kind of bad about beating out the singing children, but apparently all is fair in love, war—and talent contests.

According to Nancy Everly, aka "Lady Parfait (Purple and Red Friends Always in Trouble)," the Diva Dahlings of Seattle, Washington, take their doll, Roxy Redhat, everywhere they go. Nancy says that Roxy has been "to Portland via train, Friday Harbor via boat, Victoria via ship, to picnics, concerts, and every event we have. She sits on our tables at dinner and in my purse as we shop. Once, I left her behind at home and she was very upset with me on my return. I don't forget her anymore. Once was enough."

Roxy's cousins? Ruby RedHat (our Red Hat Society mascot) and Dollie, mascot of the Dollies in Red of Bucyrus, Ohio. Dianne Ahlefeld told us that the Dollies purchased a custom make-your-own doll with purple hair and a friendship heart. The doll wears red shoes, a red top, purple shorts, and a banner that reads, MY HEART IS FULL OF FRIENDSHIP. Dollie is already a world traveler: When a member takes a trip, she will take Dollie with her. In her first few months as their mascot, she has already been to Chicago and Hawaii.

Sometimes we find humor in playing lighthearted tricks on one another. For the organizational gathering of the Happy Antique Tootsies of Vermilion, Ohio, many of the ladies purchased their dream hats, while others opted to be creative and make their own. Linda Ackerman, the secretary/treasurer of the group, and Maryann O'Leary, the "Happy Antique Queen Mum," were two of the cheerful milliners. Linda spray-painted two straw hats red so the two women could decorate them; she repeatedly calmed Maryann's fears, telling her that the red paint absolutely would not rub off on her hair once the hat was dry. Everybody wore their glorious hats to their first event. As it drew to a close, Maryann excused herself. When she returned, someone asked to inspect her hat, which Maryann handed over proudly, thereby revealing a bright red paint ring on her hair! Everybody screamed in horror and amazement, most of all Linda, who didn't know that when Maryann excused herself, she had used red hairspray to make the ring. Linda insists, of course, that she knew all along—but they have pictures of the expression on her face that suggest otherwise!

It's fun to play tricks on one another, and surprise one another—as long as the tricks and surprises turn out to be good-spirited. Who among us doesn't enjoy a flicker of the unexpected in our lives? The Orleans Orchids in western New York State preserve the mystery in their lives by keeping their monthly event plans a secret up until the last possible moment—even from themselves! Each member is in charge of one monthly event, and the others have no idea where they'll be going or what they'll be doing until they get a phone call with the details. "Wondering what will come next is definitely part of the fun," says Queen Joan Boyer.

Some of us manage to pull pranks on *ourselves* without realizing it. Take the case of Lin Lehmicke (the Rowdy Red Hat Mamas of Northwest Wisconsin, Luck, Wisconsin), who visited Las Vegas with a group of red-hatted friends. The women caused quite a stir in the casinos, took pictures with an Elvis impersonator, and then went to dress for dinner. Lin grabbed her shoes, put them on, then headed to a friend's room for a precocktail hour drink. "I have trouble walking," explained Lin, "and I carry a cane, so I thought nothing of not being able to walk comfortably to her room." While at the party, one of her friends pointed out to her that she was wearing two different shoes, one red and one pink. But that wasn't all! She was also wearing two *right* shoes. Lin went back to her room immediately and changed into tennis shoes.

Queen Pat Dresler of the Sassy Ladies with Hattitude in Spokane, Washington, shared the tale of an embarrassing experience suffered by one of her chapterettes. Recently they took a jaunt to nearby Wallace to enjoy afternoon tea at Notions, Potions, and Brews. Says Pat: "We were all decked out, but one member topped us all with her 'cha-cha' outfit. This consisted of a gorgeous shimmery purple sleeveless top and capri pants that she wears with a sparkling purple necklace and the most beautiful sequined purple hat. While she was sitting outside the tea shop, two gentlemen from Pennsylvania struck up a conversation with her. The town of Wallace used to have a famous bordello. (It is now closed but the gentlemen didn't know that.) They asked her if she was perhaps a 'lady' from that bordello! She got quite a kick out of that and laughingly told them she was there for a tea party." Pat adds, "I might just have to keep an eye on her!"

Also seeing herself through a surprising (and amusing) lens was Esteemed Vice Mother Linda Murphy of our Fabulous Founders. She told me about a funny thing that happened to her soon after she and I got matching tattoos (more about that later). She had signed up to give blood at her church and was answering the polite questions of the nice young volunteer, questions such as "Do you know your blood type?" and "Have you had hepatitis at any time?" Then the young man asked what he undoubtedly thought was a perfunctory question: "Have you had a tattoo or body piercing in the past year?" Linda said that his face was a study when she replied, "Oh, I forgot about that. Yes, I have gotten a tattoo recently." But that's not all. "What makes it even funnier," Linda said, "is that this was the Sunday that our pastor, who has begun a motorcycle ministry, wore jeans, boots, and a black leather jacket to preach—and encouraged bikers to bring their bikes for display out front. There you have it. A biker minister and a sixty-one-year-old tattooed parishioner."

Dreaded Old Age

I have always dreaded old age. I cannot imagine anything worse than being old. How awful it must be to have nothing to do all day long but stare at the walls or watch TV!

So last week, when the president suggested we all celebrate Senior Citizen Week by cheering up a senior citizen, I decided to do just that. I would call on my new neighbor, an elderly retired gentleman, recently widowed, who, I presumed, had moved in with his married daughter because he was too old to take care of himself.

I baked a batch of cookies, and without bothering to call (some old people cannot hear the phone), I went off to brighten this old guy's day.

When I rang the doorbell, this "old guy" came to the door dressed in tennis shorts and a polo shirt, looking about as ancient and decrepit as Donny Osmond.

"I'm sorry I can't invite you in," he said when I introduced myself, "but I'm due at the Racquet Club at two. I'm playing in the semifinals today."

"Oh, that's all right," I said. "I baked you some cookies—"

"Great," he interrupted, snatching the box. "Just what I needed for bridge club tomorrow! Thanks so much!"

I continued, "—and just thought we'd

visit awhile. But that's okay! I'll just trot across the street and call on Granny Grady."

"Don't bother," he said. "Gran's not home; I know. I just called to remind her of our date to go dancing tonight. She may be at the beauty shop. She mentioned at breakfast that she had an appointment for a tint job."

So I went home and called my mother's cousin (age eighty-three). She was in the hospital . . . working in the gift shop. I called my aunt (age seventy-four). She was on vacation in China. I called my husband's uncle (age seventy-nine). I forgot . . . he was on his honeymoon!

I still dread old age, now more than ever. I just don't think I'm up to it!

—Author unknown, found on the Internet

2

Games We Play

Every child is an artist. The problem is how to remain an artist once he grows up.
—Pablo Picasso

The most potent muse of all is our own inner child.
—Steven Nachmanovitch

WORDPLAY

Once our playful sides are given free rein, we find ourselves discovering brand-new playgrounds! If we can be silly with one another, tease one another, and play harmless jokes on one another, why not play around in other areas? Why not write new words to old songs just for fun? Why not dabble in poetry? Why not think up silly names for ourselves and our friends? Why not get together and pick humorous names for our chapters? Playing with words can provide us with hours of amusement!

A lot of very talented and clever Red Hatters have amused themselves (as well as their chapters) by putting new words to old tunes, with admirable results.

Queen Mama Pat Enger (the Last of the Red Hat Mamas, Ellicottville, New York) sent a whole songbook of old favorites, all of which had clever new lyrics. Here are a few samples:

Red Hat Gal, Won't You Come Out Tonight
(to the tune of "Buffalo Gals")

Red Hat Gal, won't you come out tonight, dress like a fright, look like a sight?

Red Hat Gal, won't you come out tonight, and howl at the man in the moon?

Come on and dance 'til the dancing wears a hole in your stocking

'Though that purple gown's shocking

And the red hat needs blocking

Come dance 'til the ground all around
   you is rocking
Do a reel with the man in the moon!

You Must Have Been a Beautiful Red Hat
(to the tune of "You Must Have Been a Beautiful Baby")

You must have been a beautiful red
   hat
You must have been a prizewinning
   straw
Before reduced to tatters
You must have pleased Red Hatters
I'll bet their friends all stood in awe.

And when it came to hometown
   parading
I'll bet you always won best of show
Your ribbons and your frills must have
   caused a lot of thrills
As they envied that big purple bow.
You may once have been a beautiful
   red hat
But you sure have lost your looks
   now!

It Had to Be Red
(to the tune of "It Had to Be You")
It had to be red
No color but red
I wandered around and finally
   found
A hat for my head.

Some others I've seen
Might suit a young teen
Might even be good
For Red Riding Hood
But not for my head.

No other hat suits so me so well
With its gaudy trim, I think it's just
   swell
I've got my red hat
It suits this old bat
It had to be red!

Carlene Stanfield is the "Revel Rouser" of her chapter, the Christopher Classy Red Hatters, in Christopher, Illinois. She wrote a theme song, to be sung to the tune of "Cabaret," which her chapter immediately adopted as their theme song:

What good is fretting or living in
  gloom?
It just leaves you dull and flat
Break out a smile, let your spirits zoom
Put on your new red hat!

Put down the knitting, the book, and
  the broom
Tomorrow there's time for that
Shake off the blues, give yourself
  some room
Put on your new red hat!

Chorus:
Come join the fun, greet everyone
Come sing the songs, start celebrating
Now's the time, so no more waiting.

We've earned the right to kick up our
  heels
And give our backs a pat
Now that we know how great it feels
Wearing a new red hat!

Apparently, no song is safe from parody by Red Hatters! Barbara Lukas (founding queen mother of the Mesdames aux Cha-

peaux Rouges, Fond du Lac, Wisconsin)
wrote this parody to the tune of "The Battle
Hymn of the Republic":

We have reached the age of fifty
And it's time to have some fun
We have always done our
duty
So some freedoms we
have won
We wear our colors
proudly
In the rain and in the sun
*Red Hats are * on!*

Chorus:
Glory! Glory! Hallelujah!
Glory! Glory! Hallelujah!
Glory! Glory! Hallelujah!
*Red Hats are * on.*

New friends and new ad-ven-tures
Are what we are all about
We're the gals with lots of "hattitude"
Of that there is no doubt

---

* Insert a verb: Marching, dancing, rolling, skipping, bouncing, etc.

Add your voices to our cho-rus
And hear us as we shout
Red Hats are * on!

(Repeat chorus.)
Sisterhood is powerful
At least that's what we're told
Cavorting with the Red Hats means
We never will grow old
We wear our colors proudly
Scarlet, crimson, purple bold
Red Hats are * on!

(Repeat chorus.)
Our numbers are a-growing
All across the USA
As waves and waves of Red Hat gals
Come out to laugh and play
Join hands across the nation and
Together we will say
Red Hats are * on!
(Repeat chorus.)

The following song by Barbara Lukas, aka "Capuchetto Rosso," (Red Hat Honeys, Fond du Lac, Wisconsin) is to be sung to the tune of "My Favorite Things."

Red shoes and purses and boas with feathers
Purple ensembles to wear in all weathers
Earrings that sparkle and big diamond rings
These are a few of our favorite things.

Tulle-covered red hats and red hats with veiling
Curvy red visors and red hats for sailing
Red hats of cotton, all crocheted from string
These are a few of our favorite things.

Bridge:
We're the Red Hats
Yes, the Red Hats
Loving life, not sad
And while we are wearing our favorite things
We truly all feel so glad!

Red hats with wide brims and red hats with roses

*Red hats with ribbons and red hats
   with posies
Bonnets we keep on by tying their
   strings
These are a few of our favorite things.*

*Red hats with sequins or long trailing
   feathers
Red hats of velvet and hats of red
   leather
Neat hats and chic hats, the smiles
   that they bring
These are a few of our favorite things.*

Even classic rock 'n' roll songs aren't safe. Queen Ellen Garcia and Vice Queen Donna Fullmer (the Purple People Meeters, Greer, South Carolina) must have had a great time coming up with a parody to be sung to the tune of "Purple People Eater."

Here are a few of the verses:

*Well I saw the lady coming down the
   block
She had a big red hat and a purple
   frock
I commenced to shakin' and I said
   Ooh-eee*

It looks like a Purple People Meeter to me.

Chorus:
*She was a red hat, purple-frocked,
    happy Purple People Meeter
In your face, where it's at, lovely
    Purple People Meeter
Feather-clad, really bad, struttin'
    Purple People Meeter
Sure looked strange to me. (Red hat?)*

Alternate Chorus:
*Well, headin' south, shut my mouth,
    singin' Purple People Meeter
Sippin' tea, golly gee, crazy Purple
    People Meeter
Write a check, what the heck, shoppin'
    Purple People Meeter
Sure looked strange to me. (Purple
    People?)*

Christmas carols, too? Why not? Peggy
Burgess, "Countess of Creativity" of the
Freedom Plaza Scarlet Hatters in Sun City,

Florida, wrote this song to the tune of "Silver Bells," by Ray Evans and Jay Living-
ston:

> *Not my fox wrap*
> *Not my fur cap*
> *Not my dress by Dior*
> *Things I wear every holiday season.*
>
> *Not my gold shoes*
> *(They are old news)*
> *Nor my mink . . . what a bore!*
> *No, I'll wear something special and*
> *   dear—*
>
> *My purple dress*
> *My crimson hat*
> *That's what I'll wear, for a reason*
> *They will say*
> *Red Hatters' way*
> *Christmas can last all year!*

If famous songs can be rewritten, why not
a famous poem? Connie Japsen (the Crimson Classics, Burlington, Iowa) shared her
new version of "The Night Before Christmas" (with appropriate apologies to Cle-

ment Clarke Moore) at her chapter's Christmas tea.

Santa's Mystery

'Twas the day before Christmas; all
    through Santa's house
Not a creature was stirring, not even
    his spouse.
The toys were all finished, and packed
    in his sleigh;
The reindeer were chewing their last
    lunch of hay
To ready themselves to deliver that
    night
All the gifts that were wished for, to
    children's delight.

Santa's workshop was silent, the elves
    were on break;
They'd worked hard all year for the
    good children's sake.
The Old Gent himself was curled up
    for a snooze
So he'd be at his best for his
    "heavenly cruise"
Among all the stars in the bright Milky
    Way,

*For the annual Christmas Eve visit he'd
  pay.*

*His dream abruptly ended; he awoke
  with a jerk!
And exclaimed, "Oh My Goodness! I
  must get to work!
I have to get ready; now, WHERE is
  my cap?
I'm sure it was here when I laid down
  to nap."*

*He checked his suspenders and
  looked under his beard,
Wondering how had his favorite cap
  disappeared.
He thought to himself, Has my
  memory gone blurry?
If no toys are delivered, the children
  will worry!*

*He'd ask Mrs. Santa; he called out her
  name.
Perhaps she'd not heard, because no
  answer came.
I'll look in the closet—I'm sure Mrs. C.
Would know where my cap is; she
  looks out for me.*

*All cleaned and pressed neatly, his red
  Christmas suits
Hung ready to wear, near the shiny
  black boots
That she'd polished like the buckle on
  the belt that he wore.
(Santa's number-one helper was his
  helpmate, and more.)*

*He peered high and low, even under
  the bed.
All he got for his trouble was a bump
  on his head!
But time was a-wasting—Santa called
  on his elves
Who frantically searched all the
  cupboards and shelves.
They found cookies and candies and
  goodies galore
That Mrs. Claus had made; but no cap
  was in store.
They started to fret; how they wished
  she were home!
And just then an idea lit up Old Santa's
  dome.*

*He looked at her calendar; he'd just
  had a hunch. . . .*

And on it she'd written, "The Red
    Hatters' Brunch."
More rapid than eagles he dialed her
    cell phone;
Sure enough, Missus answered, "I'm
    on my way home.
I can't wait to tell you, but you have to
    see
What I wore for my hat at the Red
    Hatters' Tea!"

And in just a few minutes she arrived
    on her sled;
Santa's mouth dropped his pipe when
    he looked at her head!
For THERE was his cap, looking
    strangely more jolly,
Sporting feathers of purple and red,
    and some holly.
"So THAT's where my cap went; I was
    in such a tizzy;
I'm glad that you're home, but we
    have to get busy."

Mrs. Santa explained, " 'Twas no need
    for alarm;
I went on a whim, and I meant you no
    harm.

*For you were asleep, and in such
    peaceful bliss
I'd no heart to awake you, so I blew
    you a kiss.
I just borrowed your cap, but I added
    MY touch.
All the girls at the tea liked my hat very
    much!"*

*Then Santa, relieved, said, "It's time I
    must go.
Help me change the cap back to the
    look people know.
I can't go without it—risk a case of the
    sniffles;
The kids are awaiting their dolls,
    drums, and whistles."
So she pulled at the trim as she tried
    to unglue it,
But with no luck, she cried, "There's
    no time to undo it!*

*"Can't you wear it as is? It looks really
    quite chic!
And I like how the feathers just brush
    past your cheek!
So what if, My Santa, you've a fancier
    bonnet!*

It's what's IN your cap—not what is
*   UPON it.*
As your wife, I'm so proud; you do
*   good things that matter;*
And I think you might be the
*   ORIGINAL Red Hatter!"*

So Santa gave in, said, "I'll go with the
*   flow;*
But I'd better not see anybody I
*   know."*
The reindeer stared at Santa,
*   feathered cap all askew*
Then they got into harness; there was
*   work they must do!*
For he was their driver, and they were
*   his steeds;*
They were bent on a mission to fill
*   children's needs.*

Santa winked, and he sprang to his
*   sleigh with a smile*
And adjusted his cap with its jaunty
*   new style.*
He called to his wife as he drove out
*   of sight,*
"I'll see you in the morning; everything
*   is all right!"*

*As she watched him fly out of the cold
    North Pole weather
A gust of wind blew from his cap a red
    feather.
She watched as it floated and drifted
    away
To the far distant lands where the little
    kids play.
So be on the lookout, for you never
    can know;
You may find a red feather out there in
    the snow.*

MERRY CHRISTMAS!

We don't always write new words to other people's songs and poems. Sometimes we make them up entirely. Red Hatters have sent piles of original poems on the Red Hat Society theme. Bonnie C. Troxell (the Cinnamon Dandies, Scottsdale/Tempe, Arizona) wrote this:

Living Fantasy
*I want a tiara
So I can be queen,
And fishnet stockings*

Of bright purple sheen
And a red feather boa
To drape 'round my throat
And when days are chilly,
A long purple coat.

When I was a child
I would wear Mama's clothes
And lace curtain gowns
With large, shiny bows
And big high-heeled slippers
In which my feet swam
And pretended that I was
A W-O-M-A-N!

A woman grows older
In years so they say,
But inside still resides
A girl who can play
Who comes out to prove it
Whenever she can
With red opera gloves
And a red feathered fan
To sip her tea daintily
From a wee china cup—
The girl in the woman
Will never grow up!

If you still like giggles
The way that I do,
Then come home with me;
You can play my kazoo!

Queen Susan Duncan (the Derby City Ladybugs, Louisville, Kentucky) found a verse on an American Greetings card program and added the last two lines to suit herself:

I dreamed of winning a lottery
But the money never appeared
I dreamed of sailing around the world,
But never persevered
I dreamed of inheriting millions,
But no millionaire came through
I dreamed of someday becoming a
*   queen*
Guess what? My dreams came true!

CEREMONIAL SCRIPTS

The younger members of the Red Hat Society (those under fifty) must wear their lavender and pink until the day they "reduate." The occasion of the fiftieth birthday of a Pink Hatter gives her whole chapter an excuse to play by holding a reduation ceremony, which can be short and simple or as elaborate as they choose to make it. These parties are often so much fun that some Pink Hatters have been known to say that they are excited about the approach of this momentous birthday, actually looking forward to it with anticipation, rather than fearing it. Although they look pretty in their pastels, they cannot wait for the day they can wear the bright colors they have long admired on their "big sisters." Costumes and laughter are part and parcel of these events, and there is no official program, but just in case a chapter needed help, Esteemed Vice Mum Linda Murphy was moved to write a poem describing the occasion:

No longer is 50 a birthday to dread
But cause for a celebration instead.
And so we salute a former Pink Hatter
As we proudly exclaim that RED
  HATTERS MATTER!
Now gather ye round and join hand in
  hand,

*And ask that our sister, [reduate's
    name], please stand
As I carefully lift her pink hat from her
    head
To replace it today with a chapeau in
    red.
We shall drape purple over her
    shoulder
The color we wear as we grow older.
Reduation complete, we announce this
    day
That [reduate's name]'s ready to come
    with the big girls and play!*

 "Ritual is the way you carry the
presence of the sacred. Ritual is
the spark that must not go out."
—*Christina Baldwin*

The Red Hats in Still Waters of Pewau-
kee, Wisconsin, include the following promises in their reduation ceremony:

- "I promise to let my Red Hat sisters guide
  me in the ways of glam, giggles, and sisterhood."
- "I promise to read the menu aloud for any
  sister who's forgotten her bifocals."

- "I promise to let her know discreetly when something sags, bags, or droops, unless there is nothing she can do about it. Then ignorance is bliss."

And they also include "unpromises," such as:

- "I promise never EVER to wear stirrup pants with pumps, nor bell-bottoms with a fur halter top."

I DUB THEE . . .

In medieval times, a queen would award titles to those deserving special honors. Members of the Red Hat Society don't wait for their queen to do that; they bestow titles on themselves. After all, who better to decide what moniker suits me best than, as Miss Piggy says, "Moi"?

Here is a sampling of some creative titles bestowed on the members of our nobility. These witty designations pay tribute to the irresponsibilities, whims, and talents of our royal family.

Queen Dee Thacker (the Mixed Bags, Buford, Georgia) is also known as the "Book Bag" because she is taking classes. The member who gardens is the "Dirt Bag," the member who works nights is the "Evening Bag," and the member who uses oxygen is the "Air Bag." Other delightful choices? Vice Queen Nancy Willard, who is handy around the house, is the "Tool Bag." Their favorite shopaholic is the "Shopping Bag," of course. And their oldest member, age eighty-three, is the "Old Bag."

I mentioned their chapter's creativity in an E-mail sent to our members, adding that, were I to be one of their chapterettes, I would choose the title of "Trash Bag" because I love to troll through thrift stores. Not long afterward, I received an E-mail from Dee and Nancy, making me an honorary member of the Mixed Bags and bestowing upon me the title of "Trash Bag." What an honor! (Another honor I was thrilled to receive came from the Latte Ladies of Oak Harbor, Ohio. They awarded me a "Nobel Prize" for Women's Fun and Friendship for establishing the RHS—"the next best thing after a woman's right to vote.")

Following are some titles chosen by members of specific chapters:

The Prominently Purple Red Hatters:
Red Writer—takes secretarial notes in red ink
Bookie—keeps scrapbook
Money Honey—treasurer

Ladies With Hattitude—Washington, D.C.: Nancy Eller's business card reads "Bettathaneva, Goddess of Vintage Women" and shows a photo of her wearing a toga and a Viking hat with red horns, and she is sporting braids (which, by the way, she wore to our Nashville convention).

The Purple Pansies of Morgantown, West Virginia, have chosen titles befitting specific talents or attributes:
Baroness Barbara de Beethoven—plays piano
Stewardess of the Storage Closet—stores chapter stuff
Silly Scribe—records activities (when she realized she was too silly to record anything, she changed her name to Duchess of Do-Little)

Dame Purple Paparazza—the chapter photographer

The Last of the Red Hot Mamas, Ellicottville, New York, have dubbed themselves:

Major Mama—choreographs their parade appearances

Queen Mama Pat Enger's full title: Her Royal Hatness and Imperious Majesty, Premiere Purple Potentate of the Last of the Red Hat Mamas (Try to say that fast a couple of times.)

The Victorian Ladies, Portland, Oregon, count among their members:

Princess Twin and Princess Twin Two—twins who are the sisters of Founding Imperial Grand Duchess Kathy Julkowski

Marchioness of Crafts—artistic member

Countess of Gemology—works for a jeweler

Kountess of the Kitchen—avid chef

Lady of Leisure—enjoys her retirement

Countess of Quilting—is always sewing a dozen quilts at a time

Countess of Cross Stitch—spectacular needlepointer

Countess of Cosmetology—makes all the ladies beautiful!

Chapter names requiring an explanation:

Royal Chicks and a Duck—the queen's first name is Duckie

The Preemie Donnas of Jacksonville—a group of health professionals working in a neonatal intensive care unit

The Scarlet Storks—a group working in another neonatal unit, this one at St. Jude Medical Center in Fullerton, California

(These women have chosen purple scrubs and red hair covers for their everyday work attire!)

Occasionally, titles have obviously been preordained:

The queen of Rhett's Calendar Girls in Atlanta, Georgia, is . . . Sandra Queen.

Amarillo's Audacious Adorables, Texas, have:

Crown Princess—heir to the throne

Nanny of the Royal Money Bag—treasurer of nothing, as they have no money

The Royal Secretariat in Waiting—still waiting to be secretary of something

Her Majesty's Notificator of Necessary News—their PR lady

Her Majesty's Nomenclatress of Nomenclature—keeper of the name tags between events

The Royal Keeper of the Book of Scraps of the Kingdom—scrapbook maker

A member of the Red Hot Retirees, Hemet, California, Queen Martie Hobson has given herself the additional title of "Birthing Consultant," because she has helped so many other chapters get started. (I don't mean to start anything, but when you think about it, there's absolutely no rule about giving oneself as many titles as one wants.)

The Jewels of D.E.N.I.A.L., located in Missouri, chose their name to describe themselves: "dames, enthusiastic, noisy, inseparable, always laughing." Several of the Jewels are breast cancer survivors who walked in the Komen Race for the Cure in

St. Louis wearing their purple shirts and red ball caps with their chapter name hand-stitched on them. The hats were encrusted with red and purple faux jewels.

We've heard that one chapter chose the name Losers because 85 to 90 percent of their members were on the Weight Watchers program.

The Five a-MAY-zing Sisters in Red Hats, a South Carolina chapter, is a group of five sisters whose maiden name is May. The oldest sister is seventy, and the youngest was recently reduated!

Queen ByDeFault (the default is that she's the controlling sister!)

MAYtriarch of MAYhem and Madness

Countess of Collecting and Collating our Crazy ANNtics

Goddess of Gab and Gadding About

DEButante/Princess Last but by no means Least

The Rowdy Rabbles of St. Mary's, Ohio, lists among their titles:

Queen Moll—Carole Beane

Vice Mum—as in "mum's the word"

Royal Rioter—keeps them in stitches with her wit

Royal Snapper—takes pictures

Royal Rememberer—makes sure they never remember anything

Royal Serendipitus—wisher of good luck for all

Royal Rascal—chapter trickster

Royal Jabberbox—keeps conversation going at all times, making sure it's funny!

Royal Rebeler—sure to resist authority shown by anyone

Royal Ruckster—makes sure they are always in an uproarRoyal

Mistress of Anxiety—worries about everyone else's problems

Royal Unrecorder—makes sure notes are never taken

Royal Masseuse—takes care of chapter's Pains in the Neck

I'm sure that by the time this book comes out, even more creative and wonderful names will exist. Please make sure we at Hatquarters know about them so we can include them in book number three!

PLAYING—LITERALLY

 "Girls just wanna have fun."
—*Cyndi Lauper*

 "Life may not be the party we
hoped for, but while we're here we
should dance."
—*Anonymous*

Let's assume that the point about the value of play has been made. We are all agreed that it is both good and absolutely necessary. We are resolved to do it. Now all we have to do is come up with *ways* to play—just like kids.

The Sassy Red Hats of Brunswick, Ohio, took the concept of play and ran with it, literally. They celebrated their chapter's first birthday by revisiting their earliest childhood days—wearing purple baby bibs to the party and drinking (whatever they were drinking) from baby bottles. Each member brought in a baby picture of herself and they conducted a "Who's Who?" contest, with each lady having to match each baby picture to another member. (This is not as easy as it sounds, you know?) Since they were already in the contest mode, they also had a competition to choose the best hat.

Queen Mother Elaine Stamm (the Rose Reds, SaddleBrooke, Arizona) selected items usually thought of in conjunction with child's play when she was asked to speak about the Red Hat Society to the Saddle-Brooke Rotary Club. She says, "I told them I wanted them to close their eyes and not open them until the bell stopped. I asked them to think of happy things like choco-lates and kisses and tiny bubbles. When they opened their eyes, a wave of Red Hat-ters was sweeping in, blowing bubbles and tossing chocolate kisses onto the tables. The Rotarians laughed and laughed. They now know about the Red Hat Society."

The Red Hat Hotties of Metairie, Louisi-ana, very literally went out to play one fine spring day when the weather was grand. They took kites to Linear Park along Lake Pontchartrain and sent them aloft in the breeze. Can't we all imagine how wonder-ful an afternoon like that was for their spir-its?

"All I can say about life is, Oh God, enjoy it!"
—*Bob Newhart*

The Red Hat Flashes of Akron, Ohio, use their reduation ceremonies as an excuse for all sorts of play. They have written a script that goes on for an impressive number of pages. It borrows elements from every ceremony known to womankind, including graduations, baptisms, royal coronations, beauty contests, and college homecomings. They have lists full of props and a number of technical support staffers who work together to make sure everything goes off without a hitch.

One of the best memories of my childhood involves a community garden that a kind soul created in his yard in Beverly, Massachusetts. He set aside an area in his white picket–fenced garden and allotted a few rows to each of the neighborhood children, telling us to plant whatever we wanted and to feel free to go in and tend our "crops" regularly. I can't remember what I chose to plant, but I vividly remember the pleasure of squatting among my little rows and playing gardener. The Select Few, headed by Queen Margaret Webb, played gardener in Lubbock, Texas, when they planted red and purple flowers, in the shape of a hat, on the grounds of Texas Tech. Each member did some of the work, and the garden bloomed beautifully, right on schedule. On their chapter's third anniversary, the Select Few surprised Queen Margaret by formally dedicating the garden to her.

Taking a page out of the teenagers' playbook were the Akron Red Hat Mamas in Iowa. Queen Sharon Frerichs and her chapter arranged a Fantasy Prom. They originally expected about thirty-five attendees, but, as often happens when we Red Hatters throw a party, they ended up with well over twice that many! As part of a fashion revue put on by the husbands, Queen Sharon's husband dressed as a queen mother, complete with a crown atop his red hat, a pink princess scepter, purple gloves, and a purple purse. Decorations included life-size unicorns wearing red hats and purple bows. (Even the husbands were playing—pretending that they were Red Hatters!)

The Bedford Babes (Bedford, Pennsylvania), with the special help of Auntie Mame Karen Miller, revisited their teen years (the

1950s) by having a rockin' party at a barn lodge. With a husband acting as a DJ and all of the ladies dressed in poodle skirts and saddle shoes, they enjoyed Coke in bottles, ate make-your-own banana splits, and smoked way too many candy cigarettes. I'll bet they got to stay up late, too.

> "One must not lose desires. They are mighty stimulants to creativeness, to love and to long life."
> —*Alexander A. Bogomoletz*

One form of play, of course, is choosing the clothes we will wear when we are out Red Hatting. Coming up with outfits to wear to our gatherings is always going to offer ways to play with clothing, hats, makeup, and even new toys! The Village Red Hatties of Mason, Ohio, headed by Queen Shirley Glorius, brought a remote-controlled robot named Miss Hattie from Cincinnati to the Dallas convention. This little Red Hatter (about two feet tall) scooted all over the place, bumping into conventiongoers and making everyone smile. An entire chapter came dressed as red-hatted geisha girls;

another appeared as southern belles in wide hoop-skirted purple gowns. There was a Carmen Miranda look-alike wearing a huge stack of fruit on her head. At the pajama breakfast, one chapter's members wore union suits with their "trap doors" open to reveal nylon-stuffed derrieres. (We just have way too much fun at these things!)

Linda Rotterman and Georgia Levy of the Classy Coastal Red Hat Sorority designed and wore special red hats to an event in their area of San Diego, California. The hats were made of red lamp shades covered in tulle, with roses attached in the back and finials on the top. These jaunty toppers inspired a lot of compliments, and probably a few imitations, too. I guess it's true that wearing a lamp shade on your head is guaranteed to make you the life of the party.

Freeing ourselves up to play requires that we let our scowling, judgmental, oh-so-grown-up sides have a day off. Little kids never decide not to play because they are afraid that they will not be able to do it well enough. They just play! Their very playfulness is so creative; they invent new ways of playing all the time. But they don't know that that's what they're doing. We need to try this ourselves. We may be terribly rusty, but we can help one another limber up our funny bones by playing together.

My daughter spent a period of time with a personal trainer, who helped her refine her exercise program in ways that aided her in reaching her physical goals. It took me a long time to understand why Andrea, who has always been a runner and a physical fitness buff, would need to pay someone to push her harder than she pushed herself. She finally helped me to understand that she needed someone else to show her ways to move forward that she would not have figured out for herself. She had formed habits, gotten into ruts, and these kept her from growing. So, if relearning how to play is hard for you, how about enlisting a friend to help you lighten up a little bit? How about a buddy to keep you accountable and make sure you do what you say you want to do— develop your playful side? This buddy has to have authority, though. If she calls you at 10:00 P.M. and says she's going to pick you up so the two of you can go to a drive-through in your pajamas for ice cream, you have to go!

I hear a lot of women say that they aren't

creative. I don't believe it. I think that everyone is able to be creative in some area. The first problem we have is in deciding which areas of expertise involve creativity and which do not.

Some people may see a watercolorist as creative, but they fail to realize that their own flair for cooking and entertaining also exudes creativity. We need to loosen our rigid definition of creativity to take in all aspects of life.

If we stop taking everything so seriously, we can more easily release ourselves to play in brand-new areas—on new playgrounds. There's really no way to do anything "wrong" when you determine to approach an endeavor playfully. Suppose that the women who planned the party for their chapter's first birthday had decided that they would feel too silly wearing bibs and drinking out of baby bottles? Suppose that the women who decorated lamp-shade hats had thought it over and decided it would make them look too foolish? Those ideas would have soon been forgotten and a terrific experience (and memory) would have been lost to them. Whether we are doing things with a group or just by ourselves, this same standard applies.

If you are attempting to do a watercolor and accidentally drip some paint in the wrong place, play with it! See what you might be able to improvise. If it doesn't work, shrug, throw it away, and try again. Don't let it ever keep you from getting your brush wet again! Loosen your standards! It's the Red Hat Society thing to do! (Well, within reason.)

Kristin Nama (the Hat Ladies in Waiting, Pierce City, Missouri) never had much use for crafting before she had her first chapter dinner. A cochapterette brought a glue gun along and showed Kristin how to use it. She also introduced her to some other fun craft materials: metallic pens, rubber stamps, glitter, stickers, et cetera. Now Kristin finds herself making greeting cards, invitations, flyers, and more. Her chapter is even planning a combination crafting and dessert night. I would find it difficult to believe that any of Kristin's friends are "grading" her artwork. I'll bet they are getting a kick out of watching this new side of her emerge.

Everybody knows that kids just love to

play with art supplies. Finding their artists within were the Mountain Top Red Hats of Prescott, Arizona. They all met at a ceramics studio to paint on everything from mugs and jewelry boxes to teapots and pitchers. Queen Connie Ellis says that they had one of their best times ever!

The Nonpareils, located in Knoxville, Tennessee, have begun expressing themselves with music. They have taken up such "musical instruments" as the washboard, the kazoo, jugs, and whistles and they play a mean version of jug-band music. When they are performing, they wear purple overalls and red caps and they morph into Hannabelle's Hootenannies! Queen Lucinda Denton tells us that they have recorded their own CD and are actually getting gigs!

 "The most potent muse of all is our own inner child."
—*Stephen Nachmanovitch*

When it comes to creativity, the Mature and Secure Red Hatters of Calvert City, Kentucky, have lots of areas covered. Queen Sidney Milton has enjoyed making sock monkeys for years as baby shower gifts. (We all remember those, right?) She makes a little booklet to go with each one, including the recipient's name. She made one just for herself and named it Matilda. While she was at it, she made one for me! This whimsical gift has been the cause of much hilarity at Hatquarters. We all work in extremely close proximity, so each of us is very aware of what each of the others is doing. Anytime there is even the tiniest thing to celebrate (such as a solved computer problem or a funny comment), the person responsible is awarded temporary possession of the sock monkey. She then sits on that person's desk until someone else does something to deserve the honor. She moves around quite a bit and her presence on one's desk is a very coveted thing. So much joy from such a small item—made out of socks!

Queen Aileen Fields (the Rowdy Red Hatters in Palm Springs, California) has indulged her enjoyment of the Red Hat Society and totally surrounded herself with Red Hat Society colors. I would call that committment, wouldn't you? She says, "Last year, I purchased a new cranberry red car, and I have a personalized Red Hat Society license-plate holder with the initials RRH QM (Rowdy Red Hatter queen mother) on it. My mailbox is purple and the red hat is painted on it—there are even a few beads around the crown. A year ago, we started remodeling our house. The entire front of the house is lavender. One bedroom is cranberry red, another a medium purple. The office is purple."

Lois Dickson, "Queen of Turtles" of the Avocado Belles of Fallbrook, California, had a terrific idea, which she followed right up on. She had had such a ball at our Nashville convention and appreciated the women she met there so much that she decided she would attend the following year's convention, bearing gifts for all. She followed through in Dallas in 2004, presenting every Red Hatter she met there with a million-dollar bill! I got one myself and was amazed to see a photo of the Queen of Turtles herself emblazoned on the bill's face. (This has kind of discouraged me from trying to spend it.)

Sue Davis (the Fabulous Founders of Fullerton, California) has an extremely unique way of playing. This form of play may have started out as a way for her to entertain herself, but it has become an undeniably interesting game for the rest of us, as well. It is important to note that upon first acquaintance with Sue, you may think she is rather demure and very proper. She is very attractive, and there is nothing about her to indicate that she occasionally assumes alternate identities. We are never quite sure when she will decide to be someone else for a while and don the wig, makeup, and clothing appropriate to the new persona.

This playacting began years ago, when one of Sue's friends hosted a murder-mystery party and assigned each guest an identity to assume throughout the evening. Sue was to be Frieda Forlorno; her husband, Broox, was to be her boyfriend, Escobar Cartel. Apparently, this experience brought out something formerly buried deep inside her and set the stage in Sue's life for more gleeful playacting. Frieda has made several appearances now at our chapter events and conventions; in fact, we never know when to expect her.

As "channeled" by Sue, Frieda has mounds of shoulder-length platinum-blond hair and is prone to dress in faux leopard-skin or tiger-skin patterns (often both at the same time), loud colors, and elaborate makeup. She will tell you in her high-pitched, whiny voice (quite different from Sue's) that she is from "My-yam-mee" (although we think she is really from New York). Frieda is currently between jobs, having retired as the assistant of a second-rate magician named Stefano the Great. She is rather vague when questioned further about that. The last time we inquired about her boyfriend, Escobar, she lamented that he was doing time in Sing Sing for tax evasion.

Frieda's half sister, Frances Dover, is from England. "Frawn-sis" shares the same mother with Frieda but is not "keen" to divulge her relationship with Frieda, as Frances is "raw-thah" upper-crust, don't you know?

Another persona is Becky Sue, a l'il ol' country gal we first met in Nashville in 2003. Like some old-time country singers, she has extremely big hair and favors clothing featuring ruffles and bows. She confides that she has never been the same since her husband, Big Roy, left her. She and Roy occasionally get back together, but it just never works out. (Don't let Becky Sue corner you; she'll whine your ear off.)

Her son, Billy Bob, fancies himself the next Elvis. He is thrilled to have "landed him a job" at a Las Vegas chapel, performing weddings. Becky Sue's daughter, Peggy Sue, has recently run off with a young man named Jimmy Dick, who performs with a punk-rock band. It seems that Peggy Sue fell into a mosh pit recently and it took a couple of days to find her. Needless to say, Becky Sue was worried "hay-aff sick."

Last year, our chapter went to a beach café at the end of a pier for breakfast. Sue didn't show up. But someone who resembled her quite a bit did materialize out of the fog. She was wearing overalls with the name Rosie the Riveter embroidered on the pocket and her hair was bound up in a scarf tied in the front. Cracking her gum, she announced that she had just gotten off work at the airplane factory.

You know, with a member like Sue, we don't need any new blood in our chapter. We've always got somebody new!

"I have enjoyed greatly the second blooming . . . suddenly you find—at the age of 50, say—that a whole new life has opened before you."
—*Agatha Christie*

Not only do we aspire to higher, more spontaneous forms of creativity, sometimes we inspire others to go for it, too. Members of the American Beauty Red Hats of Melvin, Iowa, were gathering each month for Taco Night at a local eatery. The owner thought that their outings brought so much fun to the place that she was inspired to paint the dining room bright purple, with red trim. Jane Johnston, "Spiritual Adviser" to the queen mum, found some red hat–themed fabric and sewed curtains, cupboard fronts, and door curtains. Joyce DeGraaf, chapter "Hysterian," made a Red Hat Society wall hanging to complete the decor. "If you are ever in Melvin," writes Judi Miller, "be sure to check out the front coffee room at JR's." I'm sure that invitation holds for any and all of us.

As you can see, play is something we Red Hatters take very seriously. And it shows. I don't know of another group of women who has so much fun. Remember when you were little how your mom would answer the door and one of your friends would be outside, asking if you could play? We Red Hatters are knocking on one another's doors now, asking, "Can you play?"

3

Oh, the Things We Do

I have an existential map. It has "You are here" written all over it.
—Steven Wright

Success is not the result of spontaneous combustion. You must set yourself on fire.
—Reggie Leach

If I had known that turning fifty was going to be this much fun, I would have done it a long time ago.
—Queen Nancy Fullmer (Russian River Sages of the Purple Age, Guerneville, California

The women who make up the Red Hat Society are a formidable bunch. We cannot be stereotyped or lumped together in the ways in which many people in our culture might tend to do (if they were not paying attention, that is). Yes, we are all women; and, yes, we delight in discovering the things we have in common and celebrating those things. But within our circle of friendship are women with very diverse backgrounds. We are teachers, athletes, writers, mothers, and friends. We fly airplanes. We raise our grandchildren. We win beauty pageants. We survive cancer. We are smart. We are silly. We laugh with our friends, and we wipe away their tears.

Some women say that they've always felt like Red Hatters inside and therefore it was extremely easy for them just to jump in and get started, while others explain that it took great strength and courage for them to over- come their natural reticence or inhi- bitions in order to get to that place. Some women just woke up one day and realized that they were in seri- ous need of an attitude readjustment and a jump start to a more adventurous life. No matter where we started from, we have all arrived here in the Red Hat Society, deriving inspiration and encouragement from our chapterettes, getting involved in fun-spirited activities, and challenging ourselves to get more out of life.

And we have. The stories that follow prove it. Because no matter what your birth certificate says, you're only as old as you feel. Science has a term for this reality, which I learned about from Lucinda Denton (the Nonpareils, Knoxville, Tennessee). Lucinda's son Spencer sent her a clipping explaining the concept of neotony, a zoological term meaning "the retention of youthful qualities by adults." The book *Geeks and Geezers,* by Warren G. Bennis and Robert J. Thomas, and published by the Harvard Business School Press, contains the following passage:

> Neoteny is more than retaining a youthful appearance, although that is often part of it. Neotony is the retention of all the wonderful qualities that we associate with youth: curiosity, playfulness, eagerness, fearlessness,

warmth, energy. Unlike those defeated by time and age, our geezers have remained . . . open, willing to take risks, hungry for knowledge and experience, courageous, eager to see what the new day brings. Time and loss steal the zest from the unlucky, and leave them looking longingly at the past. Neoteny is a metaphor for the quality—the gift—that keeps the fortunate of whatever age focused on all the marvelous undiscovered things to come. Frank Gehry designs buildings that make architects half his age gasp with envy. Neoteny is what makes him lace up his skates and whirl around the ice rink, while visionary buildings come to life and dance inside his head.

How exciting to discover this word! I wonder how long it will be before the Red Hat Society registers a chapter calling themselves the Neotonous Nymphs, or some such name. Whether we add that word to our everyday vocabulary or not, the concept is extremely valuable.

"Develop interest in life as you see it; in people, things, literature, music—the world is so rich, simply throbbing with rich treasures, beautiful souls and interesting people. Forget yourself."
—*Henry Miller*

THE CHILD INSIDE

 "Take care of the luxuries and the necessities will take care of themselves."
—*Dorothy Parker*

So many of our laugh and cry lines form in response to what happens with and to those we love. We can't control any of those things; we can only try to respond with love and kindness. We do that cheerfully (usually) and graciously (98 percent of the time). But there's no time like today to begin practicing occasionally to set the stage for deliberately earning some smile and laugh lines—all by ourselves! This will include making a "just for us" list of treats—things that we don't often make room in our schedules for. Somehow it just seems easier and more gracious to postpone our own gratification in favor of the needs of others. For a lot of us, this has become such a habit that we have lost even the awareness of what we would like to do if we had the time. Let's be honest. We do have the time.

Speaking of gratification: The vehicle for altering behavior, known formally in the field of psychology as "behavior modification," can work miracles. Children can learn to do chores regularly if there is a chore chart posted conspicuously in the home, and if there is a coveted reward promised for the successful completion of said chores. Guess what? This system can work for adults, too—even if they are both the chart makers *and* the chart *markers.*

Years back, I was trying to form the habit of taking a vigorous daily walk. Of course, acquiring a new good habit can be just as hard as eliminating an old bad one. Despite the best of intentions, I missed almost as many daily walks as I actually took. So in a fit of desperation, I made myself a "star chart" like the ones I remembered from elementary school. I ruled a sheet of paper into little boxes—seven across and four down—

and wrote the days of the week across the top—thus making my own one-month calendar. Feeling a little foolish (did I actually think I could manipulate myself?), I went (walked, of course) to the drugstore and bought a little package of brightly colored foil stars, just like the ones I remembered (only now you don't have to lick them). I put my chart on the front of my refrigerator, right where my children's artwork used to go. I knew that I and everyone else who came into the kitchen would see it. The next day, I took my walk. When I came home, I allowed myself to select a star—the first one was red, since that is my favorite color—and stuck it in the appropriate box. Silly as it sounds, I really got a charge out of that.

The star chart worked where everything else had failed. Over the next couple of weeks, the stars began to march like little medals across the page and I found myself reluctant to miss any walks, since that would mean leaving a gaping white hole in my chart, there for all to see, a record of my failure. Even on days when I was exhausted or terribly pressed for time, I fit that walk in and earned my star. I discovered that, for me at least, blatant self-manipulation works.

My behavior had actually been modified. Though it has been years since I bought my last box of stars, the walks continue.

The first book about the Red Hat Society made use of this principle by including "permission slips" to be cut out and used by those who just couldn't seem to allow themselves to take a little downtime and look for fun without first getting permission from somewhere or someone else. But if those were used at all, it was probably only once.

Now, how about giving some serious thought to deliberately building beneficial new *habits* of play into your life? You *know* you can be depended upon to do the other stuff—that is, calling the plumber, picking up the dry cleaning, schlepping to the grocery store. Do you think it may be time to make yourself a star chart?

Queen Mother Victoria Jenkins (the Royal Russets, Hansen, Idaho) wrote to tell me that it is "never too late to be what you might have been." She says, "The Red Hat Society has given me a reason to want to get out of bed in the morning, a feeling of anticipation that I have not had for many years. As a young girl, I dressed up in old ball gowns, costume jewelry, and hats that were castoffs from my mother and aunts. I would have tea parties and dream of being a princess. Who knew I'd end up being a queen!"

It is exciting to me to detect the element of joyful play that comes through in Victoria's words. Playing is so liberating, and sometimes we are able to sustain that sensation and carry it over into various creative pursuits. The freedom we allow ourselves in one area often seems to spill right over into another part of our lives, in much the same way as a stream, suddenly undammed, will flow out into new terrain. Nancy J. Knight, queen mother of the Rosy Boas of Pioneertown, California, rediscovered her creative spirit through the Red Hat Society. "I am very thankful to 'be alive' again," she says, "and I know that I owe a lot of it to the Red Hat Society. It's sort of like being a little girl again and playing dress-up and tea party, but now I get to have more than one or two dresses, not to mention the fun shopping for them, and of course there are shoes, purses, jewelry, etc., etc. I am beginning to regain creativity, and have begun writing again. I am proud to be a member of the fastest-growing and most fulfilling disorganization in the world . . . maybe in the universe!"

 "The world is your playground. Why aren't you playing?"
—*Ellie Katz*

We Red Hatters love being reintroduced to our childhood dreams—and our childhood friends. Queen Bee Lynn Duncan (the Atomic Hot Heads, Oak Ridge, Tennessee) told us how the Red Hat Society helped her reunite with her high school girlfriends. They decided to form a chapter, calling themselves the TP Red Hats, in honor of their alma mater, Terry Parker High School in Jacksonville, Florida. (That's a relief! When we first registered their chapter at Hatquarters, we feared the TP might be a hint that their chapter goes out and "decorates" yards with toilet paper during slumber parties, like we did in high school.) "It amazes me how quickly, even after more than thirty years of being apart without any communications, we were immediately best friends again, sharing our most intimate dreams and heartaches," wrote Lynn. "Among the seven of us, one is still married to her high school sweetheart, four of us divorced our first husbands, three remarried, three had their husbands die, and one has lost a child. The child died just this past spring, and when I walked up to my friend at the funeral home to give her a hug, she said, 'I'm not supposed to see you until October' " (which was to be their next Red Hat Society chapter event). But friendship, especially of the Red Hat Society variety, doesn't adhere to schedules.

The Red Hat Society can also turn old neighbors into new pals. Edna Monk, the "Queen of Tarts" of the Sweet-Tarts in San Diego, California, says that she logged on to the Red Hat Society Web site and was surprised to find the name of a neighbor she hardly knew listed as a chapter queen. They had lived near each other for twenty-six years without ever having had a proper chat! Thanks to their royal connection, Edna went down the street and introduced herself, "queen to queen." Edna reports that they are building a great relationship, and that her inner child has re-emerged.

Our inner children certainly appreciate

our Red Hat memberships, but so do our actual children! The following is from an E-mail sent by Cindy Whitsett, who is the daughter of Red Hatter Carolyn Abbott.

To Her Highness:
Recently I was sent a picture of my mother. I was sure senility had overtaken her. She was in a red hat and a purple dress! All manner of decorum had been abandoned. After the shock left me, I studied the picture further. She was beaming. Her friends, also infected by the dementia, had the same gleeful expression. I realized it was not senility, but the silliness that I so often loved seeing in my mother as I grew up. She was simply impish.
I want to thank you for renewing that spirit in my mother. She is a wonderful blessing to me and all whom she encounters. I live very far from her, and delight in seeing pictures of her happy. She has spoken fondly of her sisters in her chapter, and she looks forward to each meeting. I am so thankful she has found fellowship with these women. Your society has

given this protective daughter peace of mind.

I'm always encouraged when people refer to themselves as "years young" instead of "years old." Bernard Baruch said, "To me, old age is always fifteen years older than I am." What a beautiful way to look at life. Some people, unfortunately, have it a bit backward. They think nostalgically about their youth, and the fun they had, and the fun they could have had—while today slips through their fingers. Part of this comes from our culture, which has a habit of pushing movies and fashions that promote the idea of youth as the secret to happiness. Those of us who have been around the block—a few times—know about the deeper joys that come from seeing things through, developing an attitude of peaceful acceptance of ourselves and those around us. I don't know anybody who would willingly be catapulted back into her youth if she had to give up everything she now knows and trade who she has become for the person she was then. Sure, age brings losses, but it brings gains, too.

Although the Red Hat Society seeks to

take the sting out of reaching the age of fifty, we are well aware that we now have a huge number of members who passed that age fifteen, thirty, or even forty years ago. These women are welcome in our "gang" because they are not done yet, any more than we, their younger sisters, are.

From the "You're only as old as you feel" department, an inspiring note came from Patti Cook, queen mother of the Richmond

Secrets of Aging
People looking at me will see an old woman.
They don't know my secret. . . .
Inside I am young and vibrant and feisty and full of attitude.
You can see it sparkle in my eyes and hear it in the sound of laughter in my voice.
Old age can take a toll on my body and ruin my physical beauty,
But it can't ruin the vibrant youthful beauty that lives inside of me.
—*June Holmes, Rickel's Regal Red Hatters and Wannabes, Clearwater, Florida*

Red Rose Red Hat Society and assistant program coordinator at the Adult Day Care in Richmond, Indiana. Most of Patti's chapter members "are way beyond the age of fifty. Some have Alzheimer's, and some have other health problems, but the one thing we have in common is our love of belonging to a special group. Our ladies really look forward to our outings. We get in our red Adult Day Care van and go all over Wayne County. It's such a hoot to watch people's faces when we pull into a restaurant parking lot and begin unloading all these wonderful ladies, who are laughing and having so much fun in their red-and-purple outfits. So don't think just because you're old or handicapped that you can't get out and have fun with the Red Hat Society. Our group ranges from fifty all the way up to ninety-three years young, and, believe me, you have never heard so much laughing and talking as these wonderful senior ladies have with our Red Hat Society."

Another senior chapter of the Red Hat Society is located in Bowling Green, Kentucky. Linda Coppinger, queen mother of the Royal Sassies, has elderly parents who are living in a retirement village. Linda and the village director coordinated with the owner of a local hat store, who brought hats for all of the ladies to try on. After the hat bonanza, the women went out to lunch together. "They could hardly eat, for all the attention they received," reports Linda. "The best part is that my mother, who had not participated in anything in the year she lived at the retirement village, had so much fun. She decided she liked the other ladies a lot, and started going to the dining room [which she had not done before]. She got a haircut and a perm. She is always asking when she will get her next chance to wear her red hat." It sounds like Linda's mother has a new lease on life, doesn't it?

Ruby Valencia (the Red Hot Roses, St. Paul, Minnesota) had this to say: "All through my middle and later years, I complained about having to dress in suits and heels and grumbled that one of these days I would wear sneakers, T-shirts, and jeans all the time. I would be comfortable, by golly! One day, I came across the poem about being an old lady and wearing purple. I loved it! So when I saw a newspaper article about the Red Hat Society, I knew it was for me. I contacted them immediately. I had found a group of women with whom I can have nonserious fun. I am now eighty-two years old and my major challenges are age-related, but I am enjoying life and living with my little dog, Mathilda. I think I have always been a Red Hatter in spirit!"

At the age of sixty-six, Alice Smart (Rose's Renegades, Safety Harbor, Florida) reinvented herself. Rose Incorvia, the queen of the bunch, wrote in to tell us about this plucky chapterette. Alice, now eighty-two years old, became a model at an age when most of us are thinking about retiring. Her first husband had died and she wanted to make a new start. She saw an ad for a senior-age model and applied for the job, without success. So she lightened her hair, had her teeth capped, and lost thirty-five pounds. When she reapplied, the interviewer did not remember meeting her before. She was hired on the spot and went right to work the next day. Alice's motto: Enjoy Life. This is not a dress rehearsal.

ON THE ROAD

A terrific way to reopen our eyes to life's possibilities is to get out there—literally. Take a plane, train, or automobile and explore. Whether you're going to a place where you don't speak the language or just two states over to the next Red Hat convention, you'll be surprised to see how good you'll feel when you get back.

When Jean Jacobsen (Ornery, Upbeat Crimson Hatters, San Diego, California) lost her husband, she thought that traveling would be a good way to lift her spirits, so she used a home-exchange Web site to go to Europe. Her story provides a terrific budget-conscious travel tip for the rest of us! Says Jean: "After writing, phoning, and sharing photos, I made an exchange with a couple just outside of Brighton, England. This meant exchanging not only homes but cars, as well. I found myself sitting in a car with five gears, and the steering wheel and the clutch were on the right side of the auto.

"Believe it or not, I soon mastered the 'beast,' and even drove to Brighton to meet my son at the train depot when he came to visit me for a few days! I made other exchanges over the years, and saw more of England, as well as Ireland, Belgium, New Mexico, and Washington." Jean loves the Red Hat Society because "the "disorganization" is another adventure to investigate. It seems as though so many women just have the courage to get on with it and continue living life with spirit and heart.

For her fiftieth birthday, Celeste C. Bancroft (the Whimsical Women of Windsor, Windsor, Connecticut) wanted to go to Paris. "Ever since I was a child," she writes, "I told anyone who would listen that I was going to turn fifty in Paris. I got married, had two children, worked, and had a very good life. At around age forty-eight I took French lessons and started planning a trip. After two years of trying to coordinate everyone's schedules, my husband, bless his heart, asked me if I'd prefer to go by myself. At that moment, I realized it was exactly what I wanted to do. I booked a hotel on the Left Bank, bought a plane ticket, and took off. I turned fifty in Paris, and it was perfect. Years later, my dad told me that my grandfather had given me a scarf that had a map of the Paris Metro on it. I was five and he was fifty. The moral of the story is: follow the dream!"

Another intrepid solo traveler is Lee Fitzgerald (Red Hat Foxes, Pointe Vedra, Florida), who zigzagged six thousand miles across the country. Lee divorced after thirty years of marriage and left home at age forty-eight—for the first time! She was living in Virginia and decided to drive to California. "I got a speeding ticket in Wyoming," says Lee. "It was five dollars. There was nobody between me and the Montana state line except a state trooper and I think he just wanted to see who that blonde in the convertible was."

"I have found adventure in flying, in world travel, in business, and even close at hand. . . . Adventure is a state of mind—and spirit."
—*Jacqueline Cochran*

A letter from Queen Joan Ricks of the Bo Peep Classy Lassies in Gainesville, Florida, made me hope that she is saving her frequent-flier miles! Joan is seventy years young, and while she does admit that she needs to learn to rest, she had this to say about her past few years' activities:

"I retired in 1996, divorced in 1997, had a mastectomy in 1998, and underwent by-pass surgery in 2001. After the mastectomy, I got right back into travel. I went to New Mexico and Italy that year, Hawaii and Scotland the next. Then came the bypass surgery. Six months later, I took a cruise to Alaska and even went on a level three-to-four white-water ride in Denali Park. And seven months later, I climbed Grandfather Mountain in North Carolina. I spent October and November 2003 touring Australia and New Zealand. This year I've been on a cruise to the Bahamas and to the North Carolina mountains, with three more state trips planned for this year."

Taking a page from history, Bette Campbell told us about the time she was invited to visit Israel in 1971. Although now queen mum of the Scarlett O'Hatters of Smyrna, Delaware, back then Bette was one of ten American female editors invited to tour the young country—Bette's first trip abroad. Bette and the others stayed in a kibbutz, interviewed female Israeli soldiers, lunched with female members of the Parliament, visited historic sites—and did a lot of haggling at the Arab market. "Now that I am eighty," says Bette, "I look back in disbelief at the life I have led." As an editor, Bette started a series of stories called the "Fascinatin' Forties," for which she traveled all over the globe looking for excitement, along with a group of folks who were forty-plus. "We traveled to Europe, the Greek islands, behind the Iron Curtain. . . . Later, I was named travel and food editor, and flew all over the world, writing story after story. Brazil, Hawaii, Iceland, the Middle East, Southeast Asia—you name it, I was probably there."

I'm pleased to report that our Red Hat Society conventions are bringing ladies from all over the country together. Those Red Hatters who are able and willing to sign up for adventure are sure to meet others on the same wave length, including some who are worthy of emulation. Doris Shaw (the Red Fedora Flora Doras and the Red Hat Saguaros, Gilbert, Arizona) went to the Dallas convention alone, hoping to find someone to hang out with. She ran into Lucille Trante (the Red Top Hatties, Clearwater, Florida) in the hall and they hit it off. Doris was concerned about their ability to get around the hotel, since she is seventy-two and had had two recent knee replacements, and Lucille was all of ninety. By the end of the night, Doris was exhausted (and probably inspired)—by Lucille's energy! According to Doris, "My previous thoughts concerning the results of advanced age changed that night as my friend Lucille completely wore me out. I have made a friend for life."

Traveling is always stimulating and mind-expanding. Travel to Red Hat Society conventions is guaranteed to provide fun-filled days and new opportunities for friendship. But my favorite travel stories these days concern Red Hatters who have just bumped into one another, sometimes in the most unlikely of places. "Cosmo Girl" Arlene Kroeger of the Cosmopolitans in Bedford, New York, was on vacation in the Bahamas when she walked into a ladies' room and saw a fellow Red Hatter, easy to recognize in full regalia. Arlene, who was not wearing her red and purple, was thrilled, and she immediately identified herself as a proud Red Hatter from New York. The regalia-clad woman was from California. As they chatted, to the surprise of both of them, a voice bellowed out of a stall, calling, "West Virginia!" "So there we were," says Arlene, "three women in a remote island bathroom, and all of us Red Hatters. I am glad to know that there are so many cool, wild, and crazy sisters out there." And serendipitously running into them is even better!

OLDER AND BETTER

The Red Hat Society is proud to announce that our sisterhood includes members like Bertha Mathilde, who celebrated her 105th birthday with a party attended by over a hundred people. These women know how to age like fine wine—savoring every experience, moment to moment. Bertha is the newest—and oldest—member of the Red Hot Sassy Sisters of Decatur, Illinois. Queen Judy O'Connor says that Bertha "still has her long red hair, which she wears in a French twist." Born in 1898, Bertha remembers traveling through the snow in a horse-drawn sled, looking forward to getting doll clothes as Christmas presents, and sitting under quilting frames, eavesdropping on adult conversations. And what does she do these days? According to an article in the *Daily Journal,* her local paper, "When she's not out gallivanting, she likes to play Bingo, do crossword puzzles, or watch wrestling or Judge Judy on television."

Red Hatters like to watch television—and appear on it, too! A day at an art show snagged a starring role in a Reebok commercial for Ronnie Klingsberg, one of the Nifty Over Fifty Red Hats of Century Village, Pembroke Pines, Florida. Ronnie had driven to South Beach with a friend to see some art and was approached by a man who asked if she wanted to be in a TV commercial. "I went home," said Ronnie, "and clicked on their Web site, and to my surprise, this director was famous. Cosimo Zitani has been awarded 'Best New Film Director' at the New Directors Showcase at the Cannes Film Festival." A few days later, she went to a casting call. "All of the others were beautiful people. The woman ahead of me was told to pretend to look in the mirror and prepare her face with cream, getting ready to go to sleep. She was quite glamorous, but I figured that wasn't my style. I decided to be funny. I made faces and then said, 'Nothing helps.'" Ronnie was selected to play the part of "Soccer Mom" in a Reebok commercial, an experience she enjoyed thoroughly.

Speaking of television, the Flying Nun is back! Sister Adele Mann, member of the Purple Passionates, Fort Wayne, Indiana, and a Sister of Providence, wanted to go skydiving for many years. When she shared her desire with a student chaplain who had been in the Air Corps, he encouraged her to try it, even though she was in her seventies. On her seventy-seventh birthday, Sister Adele decided that it was time. She signed up, along with a young friend, to make a jump. A neighbor called every TV station and newspaper in town. "There never was a more beautiful sight as seeing that many-colored parachute open wide," she says.

 "One thing life has taught me: if you are interested, you never have to look for new interests. They come to you. When you are genuinely interested in one thing, it will always lead to something else."
—*Eleanor Roosevelt*

We Red Hatters can boast of our very own Million-Dollar Woman. Yola Polizzi, queen of the Keuka Corkers in Hammondsport, New York, tells us that at age sixty-nine, she is a bionic woman and an active queen mother. A twenty-three-year survivor of breast cancer, she has undergone a mastectomy, mammoplasty reduction, and plastic surgery, and three total knee replacements ("I wore one out climbing hills and dancing"). "It's the fun things in life that keep you going," affirms Yola, "and The Red Hat Society is surely one of these!"

Another vibrant going-on-seventy member is "Aunty Ruth," aka Ruth A. Brown, the queen mother of the Rambling Prairie Roses in Dickinson, North Dakota. "When I answered an E-mail from a new pen friend in India," says Aunty Ruth, "little did I know what an interesting road it would take me down." Ruth's new friend was Shantipriya Basiston, founder and secretary of an organization called DAYA in the Indian state of Orissa. *Daya,* means "compassion" in the Oriyya language, and this institution for the Destitute Aged and Youth cares for lepers and orphans, as well as working for the empowerment of poor rural women.

Ruth went to India, where she traveled to Bhubaneswar to meet Shantipriya and visit the orphans. "The trip was a day's journey by car, over some of the bumpiest roads I have ever traveled on," according to Ruth. She was so touched by what she saw that she now volunteers as an adviser to the orphanage and is working to build a network of supporters in the United States. Ruth makes an annual visit to the orphanage, where plans are being made to purchase some milk cows so that the youngsters will have fresh milk to drink. "So here I am, at age sixty-nine," she says, "embarking on a new journey in my life." As soon as enough supporters are found, the children will be moved to a new building, where they will be able to receive better education and nutrition. The building has already been named. It will be called Aunt Ruth's Orphanage.

Now, isn't it inspiring to hear about Ruth's wonderful accomplishment—at an age when she might have thought that she had already made her most important mark on the world? None of us really knows what lies ahead for us; perhaps our greatest achievements lie ahead of us, rather than behind us. Let's keep our eyes off the rearview mirror!

THE MIDAS TOUCH

We Red Hatters have the secret ingredient that the alchemists were missing—the attitude and spirit to turn any challenge into a personal victory. Members of the Caribbean Palm Bonnets in Saint Thomas, U.S. Virgin Islands, sent "sunny, warm greetings" and news that member Billye Mayo won the Ms. America Classic crown in 2004. Jane Clemo, queen mother, says that "Billye is a lovely lady who wears her red 'palm bonnet' in style and with pride."

This chapter's members are still "going for the gold," whether it's a queen's crown or an Olympic gold medal. Anne Abernathy, also a Caribbean Palm Bonnet, is a five-time Olympian who plans to compete a sixth time in Italy in 2006—at the age of fifty-two! Her sport is the luge, in which the athlete lies on her back, steering a sled with her feet down an impossibly fast track of ice. She already holds the record as the oldest woman ever to compete in the Winter

Olympic Games. Known as "Grandma Luge" by competitors, she represents the U.S. Virgin Islands in competition. Grandma Luge is one tough cookie—she has overcome cancer, multiple broken bones, twelve knee surgeries, and even a hurricane, which destroyed her home in Saint Thomas—and still competes against athletes half her age. She is also an enthusiastic Red Hatter. Since she does some of her training in Virginia, she has also joined the Red Foxes of Oakton, Virginia. The "Queenster" of the Red Foxes, Penny Bellas, wonders if we "can't just see her flying down the track in a purple suit with a red helmet." That definitely sounds like a plan to me!

Another Red Hat athlete is Dorothy Vencelov (the Ravishing Ruby Red Hatters, Dearborn, Michigan). A very active eighty-two-year old, she swims three to four days a week and has set several state swimming records. Last year, she made the list of the top ten best swimmers of the Master Swimming Association, and on the opening day of a new community center, she was the first senior to scale the thirty-foot rock wall. "My talent is clogging and playing a musical saw," says Dorothy, "and I am on my sixth passport." This is not a boring woman! And she sure doesn't sound like *she's* done!

 "Security is mostly a superstition. It does not exist in nature. . . . Life is either a daring adventure or nothing."
—*Helen Keller*

Members of the Roll 'N' Red Hots of Marysville, Washington, range in age from the thirties to the seventies. This talented group of ladies skates together, performing in shows, winning medals, and taking part in regional and national championships for roller-skating. Queen Dianne Best Wildermuth says, "We care for and about one another and are a family of women with goals that require desire, determination, discipline, and dedication. We derive hours of pleasure preparing for the Marysville skating shows. Our next show will feature a number with the Roll 'N' Red Hots performing as a unit in a salute to the Red Hat Society. Our red hats and purple attire will definitely be worn. We are truly enjoying the Red Hat Society and anticipate many excursions and entertaining events in the pursuit of fun, frolic, and friendship!" Rock on ladies! (Oh, and, of course, roll, too!)

I'm also thrilled to announce that one of the original Rosie the Riveters is now a Red Hatter. Georgie Bright Kunkel (West Seattle Red Hatters, Washington) tells us that while "waiting for my fiancé to return from his foxhole in India during World War II, I drilled holes in wing panels for the B-17 bomber in little old Chehalis, Washington. One day near the end of my shift, the horn sounded and someone said on the loudspeaker, 'The war is over. You can all go home.' Everyone spilled out into the street, laughing and crying for joy. After that summer, I knew I could do anything I set my mind to." And that attitude has stood her in good stead in the many years since. Now a young woman of eighty-four, Georgie says, "It's a wonderful life when a woman like me can make a difference in the world. I am in the world and determined to live fully. I am laughing my way to one hundred."

 "Someone's boring me. I think it's me."
—*Dylan Thomas*

The Queen Mum Barbara N. DeVilbiss (the Rouge Touques, Matawan, New Jersey) spent years as a Girl Scout troop leader. With her theater arts background, she taught the girls how to apply face paint, which turned out to be popular one summer. This led to Barbara and the girls volunteering as clowns in local nursing homes. "The girls grew up and graduated, but I did not. I joined the Peter Pan Society and swore, 'I won't grow up!' I joined a clown ministry under the name of De . . . Lite, and eventually I began clowning at parties, traveling to Australia and England to clown, and teaching clowning and magic skills at the local junior college."

Sharon Lee Poe (the Gorgeous Glacier Gals, Anchorage, Alaska) has had a full life, with experiences ranging from winning blue ribbons for her baking and cooking to spending years working along with her husband for the American embassy in England and Belgium. A breeder of golden retrievers and a volunteer for the Special Olympics and the Boy Scouts, Sharon was diagnosed with breast cancer in October 2002. Displaying her indomitable spirit, she tells us that she is "continuing to do well." One of her biggest rewards is functioning as an example to others, letting them see cancer can be beaten. "I am still becoming the person I want to be," she says. "And that's why I joined the Red Hatters."

Serving our country has been an important part of the lives of many of our women. Gwen Michal, queen mother of the Blanco Red Hatted Hot Flashers, Blanco, Texas, sent us a story called "From Navy Cover to Red Hat," detailing her experiences in the U.S. Navy. When she was in her late twenties, Gwen had quit a series of jobs. Her father suggested the navy, saying, "It's something you can't quit." It turned out to be something Gwen didn't want to quit. She remained on active duty for twenty years, serving in areas across the United States and throughout Europe. She retired as a senior chief petty officer. Gwen says, "I had a wonderful, exciting career, and I also love being retired. My husband and I moved from Virginia to Texas, where we live with two dogs and three cats out in the country on our little piece of heaven." Gwen started the Blanco Red Hatted Hot Flashers to ensure that turning fifty would be a joyful experience, rather than a dismal one, and she says that she loves laughing with her ladies and wearing her red-and-purple "uniform"—a little more colorful and less restrictive than U.S. Navy blue.

SECOND STARTS

Sometimes it takes years to change your life, and sometimes it just takes free doughnuts. Some years back, Queen Mom Alice Calonga of the Red Hatted Hooters in Ellenville, New York, followed a sign for doughnuts and coffee while waiting for her daughter to finish her cheerleading practice. She found herself in a room where students were registering for classes at the local community college. After talking with a very insistent recruiter, she found herself signing up for classes, then going back to school at the age of forty. "Granny Allie" graduated from nursing school the same year that her son graduated from high school and her daughter graduated from college, also the same month that Saira Anne, her granddaughter, was born.

Three years later, Allie's daughter Paula and little Saira Anne were hit by a car as they were crossing the street. Saira Anne was left paralyzed from the neck down. "I realized that divine intervention had come to me in the form of a doughnut," Granny Allie says. "God knew we would need a nurse in the family. Saira spent almost two years in the hospital, then came to live with me. She has lived with me since 1995. She is mainstreamed in our local school. She was even the vice president of her tenth-grade class this year! She has blessed us in more ways than I can tell you."

With all of the challenges she has faced, Allie really appreciates the Red Hat Society. "The Red Hat Society has liberated me from the confines of my home, reunited me with people I hadn't seen in years, put me in touch with people I would never have met otherwise, replenished my wardrobe with color and whimsy, and, most of all, made me feel the little girl who still lives inside this fifty-plus body."

 "I could not at any age be content to take my place in a corner by the fireside and simply look on."
—*Eleanor Roosevelt*

As we keep saying, Red Hatters are not done! Most of our members say they are still in the process of becoming the women they've always dreamed of being—or perhaps always were inside. Tiger T. Jonnson-Mokuau, "Queen Heiress of the Purple-Blue Glass," is part of the Purple Petticoat Gang in the Lower Columbia Basin, Kennewick, Washington. She changed her name to Tiger—legally—to celebrate her "growth, independence, and sometimes necessary fierceness to hold my ground, to stand up and be all that I can be!" Tiger says that her "blossoming" has been an ongoing process, one that involved learning "to expand my thinking to embrace other ideas and ways of doing and being. I'm scared every time I try something drastically different, out of my comfort zone! But the rush of exhilaration after I've stood toe-to-toe with fear, looked at it eyeball-to-eyeball and walked on through as if it were a mere wraith, is wonderful!"

Marlene O'Day of the Red Hatters of North Raleigh, located in North Carolina, shared a lesson about reinventing oneself that she learned from her mother and grandmother. Both of these women started new careers at a time when most of their peers were retiring. At the age of fifty-six, her grandmother became a practical nurse. "She nursed folks in their sixties, seventies, and eighties until was she was into her eighties," says Marlene. "I don't know if she ever felt like one of the 'old folks,' much less understood the condition." Marlene's mother learned the "it's never too late" lesson, too, and went into the real estate business when she was seventy-two. She passed the license exam and was in the Million-Dollar Sales Club for the next ten years. Marlene had wanted to design clothes since she was a little girl. So, following the example set by both her grandmother and mother, she purchased a sewing machine in her mid-sixties and started to take lessons. And she isn't planning on stopping there. "With my entrepreneurial spirit," she says, "I shall surely spin that off into some type of business when I'm in my seventies." Boy, they aren't kidding when they tell us that our kids are watching us! What examples do we want to set for our children—even if they are already adults?

Alice Ryan, a Red Hatter from Palm Beach Gardens, Florida, made her first big career change in 1978, after a divorce, and became the first female correctional officer at her facility. She raised her three children as a single mother, and dealt with the challenges of being a woman in a "man's world." Alice says, "The first day there, I felt unwelcome, and that there had been pressure to hire me. For three and a half years, I was miserable. I transferred to another facility, where I met my wonderful second husband, who supported me through my real life change. At the age of fifty, I graduated from college with a B.S. degree, and five years later, I earned my M.S."

 "One can never consent to creep when one feels an impulse to soar."
—*Helen Keller*

We're all for late bloomers! The queen mother of the Adirondack Red Hats in Lake Pleasant, New York, Patricia T. Leadley, says that at seventy-two she is finally confident enough to do things she couldn't do before. When she was ten, she had thought about becoming a veterinarian, but she was told, "Girls can't do that." She married at twenty. She says, "In the nineteenth year of our marriage, I finally developed some backbone. I applied for student loans and became a college freshman, driving back and forth each day. After the initial shock, my husband rose to the occasion. Earning my B.A. gave me self-confidence! I was proud to be the first college graduate in my family. In 1991, still a sucker for animals, I set up a small nonprofit humane corporation that pays for the spaying/neutering of cats within our county. In 2002, I blossomed further, and started a poetry club, which meets at a local school. And branching out in a new direction, I started a new chapter of the Red Hat Society. We are on our way! Who knows what I will do next? All I know is, it will be whatever I want to do. And it will be fun. I am making up for lost time!"

Don't you love that phrase, "making up for lost time"? Doing it is even more fun than saying it!

Outrageous fancy outfits may have their place in the Red Hat Society. But when you are preparing to throw caution to the winds, you might want to keep the following fashion advice in mind.

Fashion Do's and Don'ts for Seniors

Some things just don't go well to-
gether:
A nose ring with bifocals
Spiked hair with bald spots
A pierced tongue with dentures
Miniskirts with support hose
Ankle bracelets with corn pads
Speedos with cellulite
A belly-button ring with a gallbladder
scar
Unbuttoned disco shirts with a heart
monitor
Midriff shirts with midriff bulge
Bikinis with liver spots
Short shorts with varicose veins
In-line skates with a walker.
        —*Author unknown, found on the*
                                    Internet

Go ahead and do whatever you need to
do to grow and change. Enjoy yourself! But
you might want to read this list again first!
Several of the foregoing stories have
been about Red Hatters who refused to stay
in their ruts and did whatever it took to put
themselves on new paths. Nobody likes to

be totally predictable, and it is kind of fun to surprise significant others, or even ourselves, once in awhile, with some behavior that no one would have expected from us (as long as it's not robbing banks or something). My vice mother and I managed to surprise each other, our husbands, and even ourselves a couple of years ago.

Let me explain. In 2001, the Red Hat Society membership was growing at a brisk clip. I jokingly remarked to three women that if our society ever expanded to ten thousand chapters (at that point, an astronomical-sounding number), I would get a tattoo. Since we had fewer than one thousand chapters at the time, it seemed like a very safe jest.

Two short years later, we reached, and flew right past, that magic landmark. Uh-oh, now what? There were certainly no shortage of opinions offered by my coworkers, chapterettes, and family members. I heard everything from "You promised!" to "You don't really think we'd hold you to that, do you?"

A couple of months passed, during which I actually visited a couple of tattoo parlors, just to see what my options were. Since the skulls, snarling demonic creatures, and even sweet little animals and hearts held no appeal for me, I continued to procrastinate. Despite occasional good-natured teasing, those around me gradually stopped bringing up the subject, and I realized that it would be easy to get away without following through. But, to be honest, my vow nagged at me. I believe in keeping my word. I also believe in the mission of the Red Hat Society. Somehow it seemed right to me to fulfill my promise.

In November of 2003, Esteemed Vice Mother Linda Murphy and I both had the chance to attend a large gathering of Red Hatters in North Carolina, put together by Queen Elizabeth Costanzo of the Victorian Roses in Wilmington, North Carolina. Despite constant activity, we found ourselves with one free hour to stroll around the charming little town. We happened upon a tattoo parlor. Our eyes met. Each knew what the other was thinking. Linda said, "I'll do it with you if you want."

With a rising sense of excitement (well laced with anxiety), we asked the young male tattoo artist how much he would charge to decorate both of us with a small image of a red hat, which I quickly sketched for him. The amount was reasonable. It would take only about twenty minutes, he said.

This was the moment of truth. I knew that if I left that shop without a tattoo, I would forever remain tattooless. I told Linda two things: I would go first, and I would pay for hers as a birthday present. Wouldn't you know that her birthday was the very next day? (Remember that it was the birthday gift of a red hat, given to Linda a few years earlier, that eventually gave birth to the Red Hat Society.)

Before I could change my mind, I got in the chair and told him, "Just do it," which he proceeded to do. I now have (and always will) a tiny red hat tattooed high on my right hip, just below the waist. (Yes, it hurt more than I expected it to.) As I got out of the chair, Linda, ever the trouper, plopped down and presented her own hip.

As we left the parlor, giggling in amazement at ourselves, Linda commented, "Well, now we really *are* joined at the hip."

And I said, "Happy birthday!"

But don't worry, I don't expect this birthday present to Linda to start a new craze.

4

Attitudes of Gratitude

Abundance is, in large part, an attitude.

—Sue Patton Thoele

The unthankful heart . . . discovers no mercies; but let the thankful heart sweep through the day and, as the magnet finds the iron, so it will find, in every hour, some heavenly blessings!

—Henry Ward Beecher

Each day comes bearing its own gifts. Untie the ribbons.

—Ruth Ann Schabacker

The first benefit new members of the Red Hat Society find in belonging to our group is

the joy of rediscovering fun with their chapterettes. The experiences they have with
their fellow chapter members are guaranteed to deepen their laugh lines. The *smile*
lines come as a result of a second, more
subtle benefit, which reveals itself a bit later
on as friendships deepen. Gradually, each
of us becomes aware of feeling supported,
comforted, and even uplifted by the caring
and kindness of other Red Hatters, both
within our chapters and within the society
as a whole. As our ranks have grown, both
my E-mail and snail mail in boxes have
overflowed with messages of love, thanks,
and inspiration. There are so many of us out
there helping one another and helping ourselves. I've realized that another thing all
Red Hatters seem to have in common,
along with their zest for life, is generosity of
spirit.

THROUGH THICK AND THIN

We Red Hatters are certainly there for the
laughter, but we're also committed to being
there for the tears. I am convinced that a
person can make almost any experience

more bearable by adopting an attitude of acceptance and cultivating her sense of humor. Unemployment, poor health, divorce, or the loss of a loved one—during our lifetimes, we will have some, perhaps all, of these situations forced upon us. But we have the power to choose how we will handle these experiences. By electing to behave gracefully, with as much good cheer as we can muster, rather than bitterly or regretfully, we can profoundly affect the ways our experiences shape our souls. And by standing by our friends as they confront their challenges, we cement our bonds with them, ensuring that they will be there for us in turn. It's amazing what a difference we can make when we learn to view our challenges—and the challenges that others face—with understanding and compassion.

Rather than discreetly looking away from another's grief, we may elect to come alongside a sister sufferer. Pat Miller, aka Princess Patty (the Dixie Dolls, Calera, Alabama), wanted to let us know about a moment she witnessed between two recently widowed women in her chapter. At a hectic planning and organizing gathering, these two women were seen holding each other tightly and crying on each other's shoulders, alone (and, at the same time, together) in their grief. "Sharing sorrow as readily as we share joy, friends for the good and the bad—I'm *proud* to be a part of that!" declares Pat. I think we are all proud to be a part of something that makes moments like that possible.

What is the best medicine in the world? The caring support of friends. When her little pink-hatted sister Malinda Koenig was diagnosed with breast cancer, Sarah Pace, queen mother of the Scarlett O'Hatters of Richmond, Virginia, put a posting on the Queen Mother Board of the Red Hat Society's Web site, reaching out to other Red Hatters. She wasn't sure how her sister would react, but Malinda was overwhelmed with gratitude for the outpouring of prayers, love, and concern she received. Sarah says, "It made me cry. From coast to coast came cards with feathers (she said it was like feathers from heaven), an inspirational bookmark, and many other encouraging messages. One card, from the Satellite Red Hat Chicks of Pennsylvania, was printed upside down, with a note saying that they would get the hang of the computer program yet." That made Sarah and Malinda laugh. Laughter is, of course, the proverbial best medicine. So this is the essence of friendship and of the Red Hat Society: the ability to laugh and cry together. Malinda carried these cards with her in her purse for a while to share with other family members, then put them in a basket on her kitchen table. Sarah says, "She feels that she is not facing this situation alone now, and if this many people are praying for her, then everything will have to be all right. What a wonderful group of women!"

 "Life is the first gift, love is the second, and understanding is the third."
—*Marge Piercy*

Deb White of the Scarlet Ribbons in Elk Grove, California, told us about the time her husband was over at a sister Red Hatter's house, helping her do some minor repairs. When the ladder he was on fell over, so did he, breaking his wrist in the process. The break was so severe that he needed to stay in the hospital for several days. On the second day, Deb found herself trying to decide whether to sleep over in the hospital again or go home for some well-needed rest. About that time, the night nurse walked into the room. Lo and behold, it was a sister Scarlet Ribbon! Deb says, "I knew that my husband would be taken care of 100 percent." She can thank that chapterette for a great night's rest.

Some Red Hatters are nurses; some are doctors. Mickey Pilson of the Yada Yada Sisterhood in Ridley, Pennsylvania, was undergoing her yearly gynecological exam, chatting with her female doctor all the while. Mickey mentioned that she hoped it wasn't going to rain Saturday, because she had a Red Hat Society outing that day. "Well," Mickey says, "she told me she was the queen of her Red Hat group—and marked my chart 'Red Hat member' for special treatment. Bottom line is, Red Hatters are everywhere . . ."

Patricia Thele, a member of Ruby Red-Hat's Ramblers, an Internet chapter of the Red Hat Society, told us about her struggles with cancer. She was diagnosed with pancreatic cancer in 1987, and this hit her husband very hard because he had lost a father and a sister to cancer. Surgery was not successful, and the doctors told her that without radiation and chemotherapy, she would not have very long to live. She rejected both. Her husband, Jerry, sprang into action. He learned about vitamins and put Patricia on a diet with no fat, little red meat, and no caffeine. "Jerry began carving crosses, which he gave to people telling them about Jesus' love," wrote Patricia, "so I know when he died in 2002, he went to heaven." Ironically, Patricia survived her husband, and with the support and prayers of her chapterettes is cancer-free today.

"A woman is like a tea bag—you never know how strong she is until she gets in hot water."
—*Eleanor Roosevelt*

Another inspirational story came to us from Elaine Embrey, one of the " 'Tween Mothers" of the Prominently Purple Red Hatters in Bay City/Essexville, Michigan. One of her chapter members, a woman named Pat Sansburn, had been hospitalized and was told by the doctors that she might not make it through the night. Elaine says, "We heard that our friend was asking to see the 'Tween Mothers of our group, and we decided that we *had* to go and see her. We were warned about how she looked and that she would not be able to talk. Being nurses ourselves, we knew that she would not be a pretty sight, but we gathered pictures of her from our Red Hat Christmas outing and we bought her a new *red hat* with a beautiful purple scarf with red hats on it, and then we set out for the hospital.

"When we walked into that hospital room, we felt a miracle was in the making. Our friend was not able to talk, but I wish we could have bottled up the look on her face when we showed her the new red hat and scarf. Her mouth opened wide, as if to say, OOOOOH! Her eyes were as big as saucers and she reached for our hands. We had all we could do to contain our tears. We told her that we were praying for her and pulling for her and that we were waiting for the day that she would be able to join us in another Red Hat function. Her husband assured us that she *would* be joining us again, and by golly, she came home after three long months. Tomorrow, we will be picking her up to take her to another Red Hat Society function at the Bay City Mall. Last Sunday, she actually walked into church with no cane, walker, or wheelchair. Now, who says miracles don't happen?"

The Na Huapala chapter in Honolulu, Hawaii, has a member named Muriel, whom Queen Muddah Leila Nagamine calls "one of our most light-filled and gracious sisters." One morning, her son found her unconscious on the floor of her bedroom. An ambulance rushed her to the medical center, where it was confirmed that she had suffered a heart attack. "The doctors told her family that she had perhaps twenty-four hours to live," wrote Leila. "The word spread quickly about her condition and E-mails flew swiftly throughout our chapter and our ladies' hula group, asking for prayers and rainbows of healing to be sent her way. Prayers stormed the heavens that night, pleading for her recovery, because she is so loved. Angels must have lined up around her bed in force, for the next morning, much to the doctor's amazement, she opened her eyes and tried to communicate. Every day brought more and more healing. The staff called her 'the Miracle Patient.' We have seen firsthand what a special bond occurs among women with a common goal.

The Red Hat Society is a catalyst for good fun and friendship, and for spiritual and emotional growth, as well. Call it what you may. . . . All I know is that we have the capacity to bring much goodness to our often-embattled world."

When Evelyn Boyd lost her grandson, the Sweet Magnolias, Charleston, South Carolina, rushed to surround her at his funeral. They sat right behind her at the ceremony and then rose to speak, as a group, at the front of the church. As they filed back to their seats, each stopped where she sat in the first row and laid a red rose on Evelyn's lap. Evelyn's sister and chapter queen, Margo Carley, says, "You never know what can happen in your lives. Your loved ones may suffer. All we can do is love them and be there for them in every way we can, every day. Red Hatting adds so much pleasure to our lives, and it truly was a tribute to my sister and her family for us to be there."

When Pat Orr (the Red Foxy Ladies, Vancouver, Washington) was diagnosed with leukemia, she came home from a treatment center and discovered that her forty-one-year marriage had deteriorated past saving. "Filing for divorce was the scariest thing I've ever done, even scarier than fighting leukemia," writes Pat. "After all, I had chosen the June Cleaver track and was supposed to live happily ever after. It would have been easy to retreat into the world of pity parties, but I began to realize that life has a way of moving on, and I wanted to move on with it. I learned that a survivor takes a pro-active role in life. The appeal of forming new friendships enticed me to join the Red Hat Society, and I cannot emphasize how much the power of friendship has meant to me on my journey toward health and recovery. I'd like to thank the Red Foxy Ladies especially for the part they have played in my odyssey. *Vive la Red Hatters!*"

Louise P. Whitney is the founder and queen mother of the Day Timer Debutantes, located at the Jewish Home of Rochester (New York). The Day Timers are some forty members strong, and Louise says that the kazoo tooting and other such silly behavior is incredibly therapeutic. Louise sent an essay entitled "It Can Be Done and I Can Do It" about the three years that she and her husband, Dennis, lived in China. Just before they moved to China, when Louise was fifty years old, she was diagnosed with Parkinson's disease. The streets of Xiamen have no traffic lights, and it was often difficult for Louise to maneuver, but she didn't let that stop her. "I did a lot of sightseeing in China and met challenges everywhere I went. The Chinese make few concessions to physically challenged visitors." However, Louise says, she found the people of China incredibly accepting and helpful. "On one occasion, the owner of a small dress shop stepped out onto the sidewalk, speaking gentle words. She took my left hand (which had pronounced tremors) in hers and massaged it, looking into my eyes and speaking softly and earnestly. I couldn't understand her, but the message was clear: I see and I care." There's a Red Hat Sister in China who may not ever know that she is one, but Louise knows.

As long as we are paying attention, everything we do contains an opportunity to learn something. Artie Morgan (the Ladies of Canterberry, Gadsden, Alabama) went to college to study nursing at the age of forty—at the same time as her daughter! As a student nurse, she was placed at a nursing home and assigned to work with an Alzheimer's patient who was reported to be extremely difficult. Along with a few other nurses, they held the woman down and bathed her. After she was dressed, says Artie, "I got a blanket and draped it over her legs and then asked her if the blanket made her feel warmer. She looked me straight in the eyes and said, 'Everybody deserves to be treated like a decent human being.' That has been the motto of my nursing career. Every time I have a difficult patient, I remember that old lady and her sage wisdom. Which only goes to show that crazy little old ladies in Alabama are some of the most intelligent people around!"

Sports stars are often applauded for showing up for their games despite injuries. Mary Holtz, queen of the Ritzy Ladies of St. Louis, Missouri, exhibited that same "the show must go on" attitude after taking an unfortunate step backward off a stage at our Dallas convention. She decided to ignore the terribly swollen wrist that resulted from her fall, but the "Red Baron" (aka Bob, Vice Mother Linda's husband) said that he wanted her to go to the emergency room, insisting that her wrist must have been broken in the fall. Mary said she would go later, if she could squeeze a hospital visit in between the afternoon tea and the barbecue and rodeo planned for that evening. At the hospital, she was diagnosed with a torn ligament and sent back with a splint on her arm—in time for the festivities! Five days later, after she had returned home, she received a call from that hospital, telling her that their radiologist had misread the X ray. Her wrist *was* broken, so the Red Baron was right after all! In any case, Mary had indeed managed to miss none of the convention fun.

When we have to deal with the loss of someone we love, there's nothing like the support of our friends to help us make it through. Queen Jan McRevey (the Heartland Red Hat Dolls, Collinsville, Illinois) says that her chapter was Red Hatting even before they heard of the Red Hat Society. When, after fighting for months, Jan's husband died of a brain tumor, she was greatly blessed by the support and care of her friends: "My friends poured in and in and in. These gals did not let me sit around and feel sorry for myself. I think we probably took more road trips in that next year than we ever did before or than we have since. When I was down, they lifted me up. There were times I think they carried me far above their heads to get me through the tough spots. We laughed, we cried, and we giggled; we became such a close group that when the Red Hat Society was formed, we knew, we understood, and were already there! We knew that 'Life is not a dress rehearsal. . . . You only go around once, so do it right the first time!' I am very happy to say that they carried me so well I have fallen in love again and remarried."

Margaret Phillips (the Royal Red Hatters, Pensacola, Florida) sent a testament to her experience of women caring for one another. "I have always felt that if you can't laugh, you might as well stop breathing. . . . About four and a half years ago, I thought that I would never laugh again. We were called by the police and informed that our son had died. . . . My friends began to come to the house that evening. They didn't call and ask. They just came."

Although they all were crying, they began to share memories of all of their boys, who had grown up together, and, amazingly, they shared an occasional laugh. Margaret says, "When I realized that I could still laugh, I felt that maybe I would be able to bear the pain that was overwhelming me. I have told them many times that they saved my life that night. They don't believe it and claim that they only did what any good friend would do. I don't think that many people would show up on such a terrible night and have the courage to laugh. They did! And because of this, I have learned that laughter heals and that we all have angels in our lives. My angels cleaned my house, fed my family, ran to the airport, and made phone calls, but most importantly, they laughed."

Our dreams sustain us and send powerful messages about who we are and what path we are to follow. I believe that they lead us to our purpose in life . . . and when we are fulfilling our purpose . . . living our dreams . . . we know that everything we have done, all the experiences we have had . . . have led us to this place. It is a profound, yet peaceful feeling . . . and one of integration . . . our skills, our passions, our experiences suddenly have a deeper meaning, as we understand that all has happened for a reason and led us to where we are at this moment in time.

I believe in dreaming big! And, in doing so, I sometimes run into people who talk a lot about not reaching so high or expecting too much and/or being more realistic. I always smile to myself as I think: According to whose reality??! We must hold fast to and protect our dreams and surround ourselves with people who support and nurture them.

Sometimes, life intervenes and our dreams may have to be postponed . . . but that doesn't mean that we have to abandon them. It could simply signal a time for reflection . . . a pause . . . and then a marvelous opportunity for renewal or recommitment. Perhaps our dreams become clearer . . . or go through a slight modification . . . and that's okay, too. What's important is to keep dreaming or keep believing . . . and when the timing is right . . . to go for it. Follow your heart, listen to your soul . . . and . . . expect magic.

—*Sara Lapides, Ruby RedHat's*
Ramblers, Internet chapter

MAKING LEMONADE

We all know the old adage, When life hands you lemons, make lemonade. There's usually a way to turn a tribulation into a triumph, if one has the right attitude. When something comes up to make you feel down, take a step back, find the ice cubes and the sugar, and turn that frown upside down. Even misadventures may make for good stories later, after all.

Queen Sharon Johnson of the Purple Roses of Texas in Atascocita used to have a favorite way to make herself smile. She would rent herself a red convertible for a day just to feel the wind blowing in her hair and listen to the music playing. She's stopped doing that—because she finally bought herself one! She even let the vice mother and me sit in it when we were passing through her area last year. Very, very cool!

A speaker at all of the first three Red Hat Society conventions, Nancy Coey, suggests keeping a gratitude journal to keep our lives in focus. She says that making a note every day about the best things that happened to you that day helps train you to keep an eye out for the good things and pause, if only for a moment, to savor them. Nancy is a Red Hatter herself, queen of the Daunting Divas in Raleigh, North Carolina. At our second convention, held in Nashville, she also coined a phrase that really caught on. Speaking eloquently about the need to release negative thoughts and attitudes, she encouraged each of us to bring to mind negative experiences from our pasts that might be the cause of our holding on to regrets or destructive feelings. Then she encouraged all of us to stand, twirl our napkins over our heads, and, keeping these private feelings in mind, shout, "Let it go! Let it go!" What a great way to perform a physical act to symbolize a decision to embrace spiritual healing! Deliberately releasing baggage, just simply putting it down, is the best way to lighten our loads as we step into the future.

Kween Karen Van Hook-Gross is from the Matriarchs of the Mountain in Allyn, Washington. One New Year's Eve, she found herself alone. Rather than stew over her solitude, Kween Karen built herself a friend—a life-size snowwoman she dressed in full Red Hat Society regalia. The photo she sent to Hatquarters shows *two* smiling faces!

"Remember that happiness is a way of travel—not a destination."
—*Roy M. Goodman*

Queen Marilynn Carlson Webber (the Seren-dipi-Tea chapter, Riverside, California) learned an incredible life lesson from a woman named "Bardy," whom she met at a church picnic. Marilynn had just moved to a new area, her mother had recently passed away, and her children were off to college. She missed her friends and was feeling rather alone, so she was glad when Bardy walked up and introduced herself. At the end of the picnic, Bardy suggested that they have dinner sometime, and Marilynn agreed, although she felt sure that Bardy didn't really mean it. So she was pleased and surprised when Bardy called the next day, suggesting that Marilynn and her husband come over for dinner the next week. They had a wonderful meal at Bardy's home, after which Bardy shared with Marilynn some advice her mother had given her: "Create your own party. Instead of moaning about the bad hand life has dealt you, be thankful for what you do have and share it with those around you. Creating happiness for others blesses you in turn. You needn't wait for a special day. For example, today I could have been home alone, but it is so much more fun to reach out and make new friends. There's always fulfilling work to be done, and new friends to make."

Lois Black, the queen of the Towanda Red Hat Goddesses in Houston, Texas, was a victim of the Enron fiasco and lost her job. She and many of her coworkers also lost their retirement funds. Instead of having a pity party, Lois started her own business, a party service for little girls, called Tea Parties to Go. The most popular party, according to Lois, is the Royal Princess, for which she takes dress-up clothing, refreshments, tea party accessories, and a birthday cake to a child's home. These little girls will learn that they can be little Pink Hatters now and, if they are very, very good, that they may grow up to be Red Hatters—perhaps even a queen, like Lois!

 "How can they say my life is not a success? Have I not for more than sixty years gotten enough to eat and escaped being eaten?"
—*Logan Pearsall Smith*

Jennifer Moyer, queen of the Tater Tarts of Troutdale, Oregon, watched her son's wedding morph from what could have been a disaster into something remarkably lovely, all because of the ability of the congregation to roll with the punches. On the morning of the wedding, everyone awoke to an ice storm. Fortunately, the guests came anyway, as did the flowers, and the food. After the musician canceled, they thought they'd make do with the stereo. Then the power went out. The bride got dressed in the basement by candlelight. She became very sad as she contemplated a wedding with no beautiful musical accompaniment. So imagine the look on her face when she stepped out into the aisle with her father to the tune of "Here Comes the Bride," hummed by the entire congregation.

Jane Aldridge, queen mother of La Bonne Vie of Steubenville, Ohio, says that Steubenville, "besides being known as Dean Martin's hometown, was once renowned as a famous red light district, so it's only fitting that the ladies of this area would be donning red hats—the bigger, the better! Our name means 'the good life,' for at this stage of our lives, we know that is exactly what we want to be living. When I viewed a tape of a Red Hat Style Show that our chapter performed, I knew what I was getting from the Red Hat Society: I saw myself stand up alone, just as I am, *not thin* (and I've been waiting for years to get thin, so I could do my thing), donning a red hat, saying, 'This is *exactly* who I am . . . this is *me*.' Our ladies range in age from forty-five to eighty-seven, and they are all obviously delighted to be a part of a society that accepts them just as they are! And my part as queen mother is simply to see that they keep on being blessed."

And just in case you weren't sure how positive we are about the importance of positive thinking, here is another example. Queen Karen Ledbetter informs us that the Red Hat Hooters in Lakeland, Florida, have the right idea. They have a policy at their luncheons to discourage negative topics of any kind. Anyone caught expressing such thoughts by their sergeant at arms is confronted with a blast from her kazoo. Then the Purple Pity Box is opened and the offender is required to make a monetary contribution. They haven't decided what to do with the money yet. But they assure me that it will be something really good!

The Red Hat Society remains a play group for women; our entire expressed purpose is to encourage our members to come out for recess. We all need those spells of down-time, and it's a fact that no one else is going to make sure that you take one. But that doesn't mean you will never find one of our chapters spreading a bit of kindness here and there. Sometimes, we just can't help ourselves!

Fun is the name for the feeling that results when you are enjoying what you are doing. So if you are doing something good for someone else, and it is something you truly enjoy, wouldn't you have to say you were having fun? Along with our love of fun comes the fun of loving, where extending yourself is as natural as breathing. The Catty Y'ats in Red Hats of Luling, Louisiana, prepared a southern-style dinner for families with children suffering from cancer, heart problems, and other serious illnesses at the Ronald McDonald House in Luling. Along with fried chicken, red beans and rice, and pralines came extra-big helpings of care and consideration.

The Red Hat Mommas of Phoenix, Arizona, have made a commitment to support their community and do one wonderful thing for others each year. The first year, they made sixteen quilts for children living at a local shelter. The ladies presented the quilts and an Easter basket to each child and each mom. Then the Red Hat Mommas went out for a lovely lunch together.

A new twist on birthday clubs: The Passionate Purple Personalities of Denison, Texas, and their queen mum, Pamela Henley, decided to honor the birthday girl in their chapter by making a difference by donating to a charity. Queen Pamela had already created a scholarship to honor her son, a survivor of a brain injury, at the Smith Center for Therapeutic Horseback Riding, serving handicapped children and adults in the Sarasota area of Florida. Each month, the chapter passes around the "birthday box" and each member contributes whatever amount she would like. The money collected is donated to the scholarship fund.

"Although the main goal and purpose of

Red Hatters is to have fun," wrote Queen Mum Peg Dunn-Snow from Fort Lauderdale, Florida, "once in awhile one of our members initiates a special service project and asks for volunteers to participate. The latest project of Les Mesdames en Rouge is Operation Stephanie. Stephanie is a major in the U.S. Army and is currently stationed in Kuwait. Her twin sister, Kathryn, has mailed sixty-five Operation Stephanie packets to family and friends, asking them to write letters or E-mail, and send small gifts to Stephanie while she completes her second year of duty in the Middle East. One of our chapter members was a professor of Kathryn's when she was at the university, which is how we got involved. We took charge of four of the packets, and we're going to get them mailed in time for her birthday. What a wonderful story of sisterly love." And a most appropriate place for Red Hat Society members to add their two cents (well, undoubtedly a lot more than that).

 "Become the change you want to see—those are words I live by."
—*Oprah Winfrey*

The Dazzling Daisies in Forty Fort, Pennsylvania, wear red hats with daisies on them and have a kazoo band. "We go to nursing homes to play our kazoos and sing along with the audience," said Queen Jean Bryan. "We love to see the audience smile." It does seem to me that it is nearly impossible to keep from smiling in the face of an enthusiastic kazoo band. This has to be one of the silliest sounds there are.

One Red Hatter who always manages to save the day is Donna Sue Harper (the FUNtastik Red Hatters, of China Spring, Texas). Acccording to Queen Mother Suzie Orner, "Donna loves to travel, and I really believe there isn't a place on earth she won't go . . . and on a moment's notice. She volunteers for the Red Cross, doing whatever she can to aid and rescue storm/disaster victims. She missed our annual Christmas party because she was going to Guam to volunteer. I remember that one morning when we were on our way to see a performance at a local theater, there was a huge rainstorm. Joan, another Red Hat sister, had worn slip-on sandals, and so she was practically barefoot in that terrible weather. By the time we reached the theatre, she was miserable and wet. Donna took one look, reached into her purse, and pulled out a pair of house slippers. I couldn't believe it! We had a ball that day, in spite of the weather. And I truly think that everything in the free world can be found in Donna's purse!"

On her way to deliver some groceries on behalf of her pastor, Evelyn Gentry (the Blue Grass Red Hat Society, Lexington, Kentucky) had $326 in her wallet. She was planning to use the money to buy groceries for herself and some gifts for her daughter's bedroom: a bedspread with quilted flowers and some pink wallpaper. She was quite sure of what she wanted. When she arrived at the home to deliver the groceries on behalf of her church, she learned of a pressing emergency in that home. So she gave three hundred dollars to help with this additional need. With the twenty-six dollars she had left, there was little chance that she would be able to make the purchases she had planned. As she headed home, she passed by a garage sale. While browsing (how many of us can pass up a garage sale right in our path?), she discovered some rolls of wallpaper, so she decided to buy them. As she looked at the wallpaper, she noticed a large plastic package. It was the bedspread she had envisioned! The homeowner explained that she had purchased it for her bedroom but that her husband had wanted a different color.

"Just give me twenty dollars for it," she said. With the six-dollar tag on the matching wallpaper added, the total was exactly the amount Evelyn had in her purse! When Evelyn got home and opened the wallpaper, she was amazed to find that it was the very print she had been planning to buy—pink and white stripes with a flower motif. "I know God could have just asked me to give my money without giving me anything in return," says Evelyn, "but every detail of the whole scenario was planned to teach me a valuable lesson, one I will never forget."

Sometimes unexpected kindnesses are offered to us, and it is our pleasure to accept them gracefully and graciously. "It was an early June day and I was looking over the selection of plants at a local garden shop," writes Judy Walsh (Etowah, North Carolina). "I was choosing between a salmon-colored rose bush and a display of marigolds. Because I was the single mother of six, I really could not afford to buy both plants. The marigolds would put a lot more color in my garden for less money, so I reluctantly replaced the rose bush and went to buy the marigolds. In the parking lot, a man tapped me on the shoulder as I was putting the flowers into my car. He was pushing a cart with a lot of petunias and *my* rosebush in it. He asked if I had a lot of room to plant flowers. I told him that I did, and he said that he used to have a lovely garden but now lives in a nursing home, where he has only a window box. He picked up the salmon rosebush and said that he had seen me putting it back, and that he would give it to me if I would do him the favor of planting it in my garden. I thanked him and kissed him on the cheek. He told me that he was recently widowed, after fifty-five years of marriage, and that his name was Timothy. I took the flowers home and planted them in my garden, telling everyone who admired the beautiful salmon-colored roses that they were Timothy roses."

Carol Adelman is a member of the Scarlet Widows in Dearborn, Michigan. Forty years after she graduated from high school, she still gets E-mails from old school friends. Not long ago, she learned that Kathy, one of these friends, was fighting cancer. Carol decided to share the Red Hat Society idea with her. "I wanted Kathy to feel what I felt,"she wrote, "to see how wonderful and attractive you feel in a red hat." She bought a soft straw hat, painted it red, and covered it with flowers and red netting. "Kathy wrote me beautiful stories of being stopped by people in her town who just had to tell her how beautiful she looked. Kathy shared the concept with a friend of hers, who was also suffering from cancer. Carol gladly made one for Kathy's friend, as well. Kathy is doing well now. Her friend, who was not as fortunate, wore her red hat to the end.

So many women have written letters to us about loved ones who have passed away. We have all lost people we love, and we have all grieved. Our members talked about dear friends, about darling sons and daughters, about their beloved husbands and their Red Hat sisters. Many Red Hatters wrote to us to share their precious memories of those they have lost. Since our love for those who have passed away stays, full-blown, within our hearts, it seems fitting that we tell our new red-hatted friends about them, which helps them to understand who we are and what we have been through.

Phyllis Poirier remembers that she was standing at the grill in the coffee shop where she works when her daughter Cherie came in and said, "I have cancer." "Strangely, the first thing I thought of was another day seventeen years ago," writes Phyllis, who is a member of the Lips'n'Hips in Port Charlotte, Florida. "I was standing in the bathroom, brushing my teeth, when the door burst open. She was standing there, my sixteen-year-old child, crying 'Mom, I'm pregnant.'" A number of years later, the same daughter told her mother that she had been diagnosed with cancer. "My sixteen-year-old had blossomed into a woman of indomitable strength. Her eyes were filled with determination. With a quiet intensity, she said, 'Don't worry, I'll beat this.' The next day, we began a long and painful journey. She was so brave, and I loved her for her strength. In October 1997, she had suffered enough. My child, my friend, and my confidante lost her valiant battle for life. She slipped away. Those who came to mourn told us truly beautiful stories of her acts of kindness. Tears still come when I speak of it, but I know that Cherie, our new angel in heaven, is smiling down on all of us."

In memory of a dear friend named Pat, Janet Cooke (the Lunch Bags, Orlando, Florida) wrote the following: "When I was in the fifth grade, a new girl moved into my neighborhood. Even though she was a grade ahead of me, we became good friends. We spent our teen years together: we giggled, went to the movies, talked about clothes, and, of course, boys, and spent many weekend sleepovers together. We both became engaged the same summer and married within a month of each other. I was her maid of honor, and she was my matron of honor. After the birth of our first babies—both girls, born four weeks apart—Pat and her family moved to another part of the state. We were both busy raising our families, but always we kept in touch. By the late eighties, we both had empty nests and I had moved to Florida. Pat asked one day if I had ever read the poem 'Warning.' Read it? I had it framed and hanging in my bedroom. We had always said that when we were old, we'd sit on the porch together and gossip about the neighbors. . . . Now we added in the part about wearing purple dresses. A couple of months after Pat passed away, I was invited to join the Red Hat Society. Of course I said yes. I guess I really joined in memory of Pat, and I know she's there with me at every fun-filled Red Hat Society event. I'll bet she even giggles, looking at her girlhood friend, Janey, all dressed up in purple and wearing a red hat."

"Life does not cease to be funny when people die any more than it ceases to be serious when people laugh."
—*George Bernard Shaw*

From Billy Hale, (the Lexington Scarlett O'Hatters of Tennessee) comes a story of how she learned to cope during the saddest time of her life. Billy is a Gold Star Mother; her son, James Lee, was killed in action in Vietnam in 1968. "He had pulled his time," wrote Billy. "He was on his way home when he was asked to do one more rescue to help some wounded American soldiers. The mission was successful—twenty-eight men were rescued—but my son and two other men were killed. My life seemed to have stopped that day, and for years I just plodded along." Recently, Billy joined the Red Hat Society. "We are without a doubt one of the happiest chapters around," says Billy. "This is the best thing that has happened to me in years. I will say we are beautiful in hats of red in all shapes and sizes. I am going to be seventy-seven this year and I feel years have slipped away when I am with the girls. I feel I am doing just what my son wanted me to do. Life is not worth living if we close ourselves away."

A letter came from Queen Mother Wilma Day (the Daring Audacious Yakety-Yaks of Oak Ridge/Conroe, Texas) about her mother-in-law, also named Wilma. "She was a flapper, loved wearing hats, and was a gracious hostess, whether the event was a formal dinner or a backyard picnic. Married to an important member of the Mexican government, she was prim, proper, and, at the same time, fun-loving and capricious. When I married her son, she informed me that her name was Wilma, that she had been there first, and that no family is big enough for two Wilmas. My new name, she informed me, was 'Junior.' Because I adored her, I graciously accepted the nickname. I sincerely considered it a compliment.

"On one of her visits to the States, she and I had lunch at a lovely restaurant. After lunch, she said we must go to the mall, since she needed new drawers. She led the way to the lingerie department and held up a pair of underwear that would have fit a woman ten times her size. Before I could say anything, she said, 'Junior, be honest. Are these my size?' The aisle was filled with clerks and customers who could not stop laughing. When our middle daughter chartered her Red Hat chapter, she chose the name Toby's Red Hat Angels of the Society of Hats in her honor. You see, when the first grandchild was born, Wilma told me that she was too young to be a grandmother and that the kids should call her 'Toby.' Toby was a mule on her father's farm in Alabama, and her sisters were forever telling her that she was as stubborn as that mule. She proved them wrong. She was kind, loving, caring, and a barrel of *fun*. If she were living, she would certainly be wearing purple and a red hat!"

When the queen of the Crimson Classics in Marshall, Michigan, passed away, the group decided to reorganize and rename the chapter after their beloved queen. The group is now called the Frie Spirits, after their friend Kathy Frie. Kathy wrote her own obituary, and the last line was "Live, love, laugh," which the Frie Spirits have adopted as their motto. "This woman lived her life to the fullest until the last breath," Queen Pat Sheets told us. "We are glad for the lessons that she taught us about our 'little kid' selves."

The Red Hat Mommas of Bucks County in Feasterville, Pennsylvania, got their start in memory of one member's sister. Queen Esther Fox writes, "My closet is aglow with red and purple and I love it! When I turned fifty, my sister Iggy had a surprise birthday party for me. Everyone at the party wore purple, and the 'Warning' poem was posted on the mirror. It was so much fun—we were ahead of our time! I think my sister knew about our chapter before we even did. . . . When she passed away, six friends and I decided to start a Red Hat Chapter in her memory. She had a hat collection—and imagine our amazement when we found seven red felt hats. We now share those!" How incredible that she had exactly the right number of red hats! We in the Red Hat Society have actually gotten used to such magical stories about serendipitous events. We call them Scarlet Sparkles!

Another special reminiscence comes from Linda Daniels (the Geraldine Go Getters, Geraldine, Alabama), who wrote to us about her dear friend Ornella, an Italian woman she met in California. "We became fast friends," Linda says. "We shared many days riding in her red convertible, top down, of course. We thought we were cool, even though we both had grown kids. She taught me how to make spaghetti sauce with fresh tomatoes and garlic, and we loved to go out for a day of shopping, dining, and wine tasting, sharing our secrets and laughing. We both lived as though any day could be our last—with a zest for life. Ornella died of cancer a few years ago." Linda says that Ornella's spirit was never broken, and she suspects that somewhere, somehow, she is "still riding around in her red convertible, having a good time."

Evelyn Gentry sent in a tale she called "My New Friend." Evelyn (the Blue Grass Red Hat Society, Lexington, Kentucky) met Anita at a weeklong government internship program, and invited her to a Red Hat Society luncheon. "She was so excited to meet new ladies, as her family had moved here from another state. Our monthly luncheons became such an important part of her life. She had lung cancer and was undergoing radiation therapy, but she still attended to the luncheons, sipping tea and talking with us. Anita passed on quietly at home. Her friend from another state told us at the funeral home that she had started a new Red Hat Society group in her town as a result of Anita's fun stories about the Blue Grass Red Hat Society."

Pat Barnett (the Red Hat Goddesses, Melbourne, Florida) told us about one of her Red Hat sisters, Dee. When Pat joined the Red Hat Society, she was at a low point in her life, having just left behind her family and friends to move to a new place. When she heard about the Red Hatters, she went to a gathering. "It wasn't easy venturing out and entering a room where I knew no one," she says. "But in less than an hour, I was so glad that I had. Two women in the room particularly stood out, and I found out that they were sisters. One of them was Dee, and she and I became friends. A year after I met Dee, she was rushed to the hospital. She was in the ICU and only immediate family could see her. A few days later, she passed into the arms of God. I was beside myself with grief and could think only of the plans we hadn't accomplished yet. At her memorial service, her red hat was on display. Her family told me that she enjoyed every minute she spent with all of us. I thank the Red Hat Society for bringing us together and for giving her the chance to laugh a little more and have a little more fun. I'll always hold my Red Hat sister Dee dear to my heart."

The "Maddest Hatter" of Ruth's Rebels in Poughkeepsie, New York, let us know a bit about the incredible woman after whom their group is named. "Our chapter is named after a woman we all knew," writes Cindy Primeau. "She was the embodiment of the Red Hat, never afraid to go anywhere or do anything because of her age. I remember her pictures from a cruise through the Panama Canal. Disney World was her special place, where she would return time and again with her kids and grandkids. She was the first to offer a hand, a little piece of her heart, or whatever was needed to make somebody happy. Her sense of fun was so infectious! She always had something kooky to wear for holidays, or sometimes just for the joy of it. Ruth was a gifted writer, and she was always writing beautiful notes and letters, which we all still cherish. Ruth was taken from us in January 2003, but even as she was nearing her end, her thoughts were of others. I talked to her that Christmas, and she was still laughing and trying to make everyone feel 'not so bad' about the inevitable. When we held our first meeting, it was on the one-year anniversary of her death. We drank to her memory and unanimously agreed that Ruth would have been the first person to join this group. She is always in our hearts. And so we named our group Ruth's Rebels, in honor of this re-markable woman."

One woman decided to learn how to grieve in order to help her family deal with her sister's death. "My sister Grace was a vibrant young woman, a mother of four, so full of love and life," writes Loretta Di Gennaro. Loretta is a member of the Almondjoy chapter in Alexandria, Virginia. "She always had a laugh to share and a hand to extend to anyone in need. Thanksgiving arrived three weeks after Grace's passing, but nobody could talk about it. With Christmas just around the corner, I went to a seminar on holiday grief at the local hospice center. As we sat down for Christmas dinner, I presented a memory candle, lighting it and explaining that we were commemorating Grace's life, not her death. I asked everyone to share a memory. I began by recalling and imitating how my sister would always run out in her bare feet as soon as it started to snow, waving her arms in the air and yelling, 'It's snowing!' As the candle glowed, this family, whose laughter had been silenced by the darkness of grief, was laughing and crying together."

Many of us may think that laughter in the midst of grief is inappropriate or odd. But those of us who have lost loved ones know that sharing humorous memories, even in the midst of anguish, can lift the wounded spirit, if only for a moment. I recently flew to Texas for the funeral of my cousin, Dallas Byers. As various mourners got up to speak, the memories they shared held common threads, some of which caused us to smile through our tears. Many years back, Dallas had had a pair of red shorts, which he wore until they were literally unwearable. He was able to find a similar pair to replace them, and another pair after those wore out. The red shorts came up again and again in the eulogies that day, and for a moment this reminder of Dal's gentle, humorous ways enabled the mourners to feel close to him, and to one another. There were smiles everywhere and even a few giggles. Those who are able to find and enjoy the occasional bright spot amid grief are those brave enough to face the harshest realities of life in the most positive way possible.

We have been so glad to be there for our red-hatted friends through their dark times, and we have found that we can be there for our countrymen, too. If offered tastefully, a splash of color and joy is never inappropriate.

A chapter in Port St. Lucie, Florida, had a gathering scheduled for September 12, 2001, which they canceled out of respect for our grieving nation. But after a week went by they felt the need to reach out to one another for support and comfort. When they gathered at a restaurant for dinner, they wanted to begin the meal with a gesture of solidarity, so they stood around the table, joined hands, and sang "God Bless America." The restaurant and adjacent bar became momentarily silent. Then the other patrons joined in the song. As they finished, everyone cheered, clapped, and exchanged hugs.

Connie Zack of Bradenton, Florida, was on her second outing with the North to South Snowbirds on the morning after the war with Iraq had begun. The ladies were feeling sad and a bit guilty, wondering if perhaps they should refrain from having fun on such a solemn day. As they waited for their trolley, they were overwhelmed by the number of people in passing cars who honked, grinned, and waved at them—male and female, young and old. One woman asked to take their photograph. A man from New York City said that they had made his day. The trolley driver even stopped traffic so that he could take their picture. As Connie says, "There is never a bad time to spread a little joy and cause a few smiles."

The Red Fedoras of Chesterfield County,

Virginia, along with women representing twelve other area chapters (105 women in all), went to Washington, D.C., to see the cherry blossoms. Queen Mother Barbara Rowe wrote, "We all had a grand time meeting and making new friends and spending the day together. The highlight of the trip occurred at a rest stop en route home, where we encountered a motor coach of young men and women who were just returning from their tour of duty in Iraq and were on their way home. Needless to say, it was a very emotional encounter for the Red Hatters as well as for these men and women. They did not know what a Red Hatter was, and when they saw us coming at them in such big numbers, they were overwhelmed, to say the least. We hugged and embraced each and every one of them, and they were thrilled to see us in all our purple outfits and lavish red hats. A few Pink Hatters were present, as well. This is a trip we shall never forget, and we're still talking about it."

Grande Dame Mary Ann Taylor of the C.L.I.F.F.S. (Classy Ladies Intentionally Forgetting Fashion Sense), in Greer, South Carolina, heard a lovely story when she volun-

teered to help another chapter plan a celebration of Red Hat Society Day (April 25) at
the local mall. She went to meet the public
relations contact at the mall, wearing her
purple dress and Red Hat Society pin. At
the customer-service booth, the receptionist took one look at her and asked if she was
a Red Hatter, telling Mary Ann that she was
so thankful for the Red Hat Society because
of how it had helped her mother. When her
father passed away, her mother had been
deeply despondent. She had just stayed indoors, letting time pass, until one of her
friends dragged her to a Red Hat Society
meeting. From that day on, her mother literally came back to life!

Just hearing that story made Mary Ann
smile. Because we are all part of this sisterhood, each of us can share in the pride of
being part of something so positive, which
is beneficial to so many. And we can continue to search for ways to encourage and
support others wherever and whenever an
opportunity arises. We matter all right, in
more ways then we can possibly know.

5

Friends 4 Ever

You can only be young once. But you can always be immature.
—Dave Barry

The best mirror is an old friend.
—George Herbert

No man is the whole of himself. His friends are the rest of him.
—*Good Life Almanac*

As we have gotten older, we have learned a lot about human relationships. Many of us have had our share of friendships or marriages that ultimately failed, and we absorbed just how much that kind of loss can hurt. But rather than dwell upon our losses, we have learned to treasure those relationships that have succeeded, standing the test of time. We also remain ready and willing to entrust our hearts to new friends. We women know that it is only within the context of relationships that we truly grow and learn as people.

There are few things as joyous as a reunion of old friends, and few emotions as exhilarating as the excitement of meeting new people and discovering we have much in common with them. This is what happens within the context of the Red Hat Society. In this vast universe, we are kindred spirits; we come to recognize one another from the jaunty angles of our red hats and the friendly eyes and cheerful smiles beneath those feathered or bejeweled brims. We are the women of the Red Hat Society, and we have come to cherish our girlfriends, viewing them as members of our extended families.

START HERE

The Red Hat Society continues to add hundreds of new chapters every week. This phenomenon has inspired us to refer to our amazing growth as "Red Spread." There are so many reasons that women give when explaining what led them to start chapters of the Red Hat Society: moving to a new area, wanting to join but not having a chapter nearby, and finding new ways to enjoy old friends. Once women have experienced the joys of the Red Hat Society sisterhood, they find themselves encouraging the women they know to get involved themselves.

My vice mother, Linda Murphy, shared a story with us that is straight out of her fortieth college reunion. "When we were coeds in the early sixties" she said, "sororities and fraternities were a big part of campus life, and, of course, there were friendly rivalries. My sorority, Alpha Sigma Chi, had such a one with Alpha Delta Eta. It was great fun to return forty years later and hook up with one of my own Alpha Sig sisters and eleven sisters from Alpha Delta." It was Linda's husband, the Red Baron, who brought up the subject of the Red Hat Society while they were together. By the time they all left, the Alpha Delta girls of '64 had decided to start a chapter. Thank you, Red Baron!

One Red Hatter told of helping her housekeeper start a chapter of the Red Hat Society. The housekeeper wanted to have a chapter of her own but was very intimidated by the idea of starting one herself. In the spirit of friendship, her employer hosted a tea for her own chapter and included the housekeeper's friends. It turned out to be a wonderful, unifying experience for everyone.

"Shared laughter is love made audible."
—*Izzy Gesell*

Marlene Duffy, queen mother of the Kenai River Red (some Pinks) . . . and we ain't Salmon, a chapter in Kenai, Alaska, started her group after returning home from a visit to Arizona. While down south, she had visited a flea market and bought a purple jumper and a red hat, red shoes, and red-purse appliqué just because she thought the motif was cute. The friend she had been visiting asked if she had ever heard of the Red Hat Society, and when Marlene answered that she hadn't, her friend explained it to her. When Marlene got home and checked our Web site, only to discover that the closest chapter to her was ninety miles away, she decided to start a chapter in Kenai. Five months later, Queen Marlene told us, she took in her eighty-sixth member. "It never ceases to amaze me how infectious this phenomenon has become here in our community. Every event we attend attracts a few more ladies to our group. It's absolutely the most rewarding experience I've encountered in many, many years!"

Joining the Red Hat Society has made a difference in so many women's lives. Connecting with women in our communities, making new friends in faraway places, and getting out and having fun—this is what it's all about. The Red Cosmopolitans are from Maplewood, Minnesota. "Queen Cosmo," aka Stephanie Layer, says that she has a great group of Red Hatters. "I have a very rare lung disease," she told us, "and this red hat stuff changed my life. At times, I even forget that I am sick. Boy, is that a treat! I am so busy with planning luncheons and finding silly gifts for the girls, who have brightened my life with the warm glow of RED from their hearts."

Over the course of her life, Queen Jean Hedrick (the Red Hat Society Gals, Whittier, California) has traveled to the Ukraine several times and become friendly with a woman named Larissa. Jean challenged

Larissa to start a chapter in her hometown in the Ukraine. While on a visit in the States, Princess Larissa encountered members of the Red Hat Society and bought herself a red hat. Upon her return home, she sent a letter, which Jean was moved to share with us. Because Larissa's English is awkward, I have paraphrased her letter: "I was over-joyed to read more about the Red Hat Soci-ety, as I liked the idea very much. And I en-joy my red hat immensely! Do I understand correctly that this is for women who feel free at last to express their best selves in a funny and witty way? I see it as more than just an opportunity for good times spent with inter-esting and 'outrageously courageous' and wise women, who are not afraid to stand out. I wish there was such a society in the Ukraine, but our women are very burdened and many of them must struggle just to get food and clothing at a time when their strength is not what it was. They are still working hard in the gardens to provide veg-etables for their families. This is a sad real-ity. I see how my mom and her friends live. Their only relaxation takes place on Sun-days, when they get to go to church and re-frain from working physically in the fields.

Because of this, I would like to brighten their lives with red hats! That would be great! Perhaps you and I together can figure out a way to start a chapter here in the Ukraine."

Letters like these really remind us to appreciate our blessings not just materially but in so many other areas. While we all have our own troubles and struggles, most of us are not out working in the fields. And we do find ourselves in situations for which there is much to be thankful. Let's all hope that our spirit spreads to our sisters everywhere possible. And let's be proud of the concepts and attitudes that we are all trying to share with them as generously as we can.

My sister, Jane, and my daughter, Andrea, are both enthusiastic gardeners. The two of them love to share plant cuttings, and each of them has plants in her yard that are descendants of cuttings they have exchanged with each other. New friendships can grow in a similar way. A quilter may introduce a friend she made in her quilting group to a friend she made at work, and those two may develop a relationship of their own, based on other things these two have in common. (Perhaps they discover they are both very interested in painting.) The Red Hat Society functions in this same way. We share pieces of our lives with others, and bring old friends together with new friends. And our new friends do the same for us. New connections and friendships are the welcome results. The analogy doesn't stop there; these budding friendships require nurture in much the same way as do budding plant shoots. Both need time and nourishment to grow.

Bringing people together is the specialty of the Red Hat Society. "Lady Cranberry" (Jo Elliot) and "Lady Di Red Hat" (Dianne Davis), both queens of their own chapters, work at Red Hat Society Hatquarters. Both are redheads and both are of Scottish descent. With these things in common, they like to go together to the annual Scottish Festival and Games at the Orange County Fairground, here in Southern California. Each of the sixty Scottish clans attending puts up a tent, which contains an informative display relevant to that particular clan and its heritage. During the last such event, Jo and Dianne were approached for help in starting a Red Hat Society chapter comprised of women from the various clans.

They plan to call it the Red Hat Celtic Warrior Women and have already created a logo for it containing red battleaxes. They will wear purple kilts, and, instead of a queen, they will have a chieftess. Jo says that the Red Hat Society has managed to do what the British were never able to: bring all the clans together!

Where the Red Hat Society is concerned, age is no barrier. Our chapters have welcomed large numbers of women under fifty into their ranks. Lois Lund, "Queen Lady Scarlet" of the Queen City Red Hats in Helena, Montana, sent a story that demonstrates this openness. When the chapter was out having lunch one day, a young lady who had noticed their red hats and purple clothing approached their table to ask what the celebration was all about. "We told her we were celebrating being over fifty and truly enjoying this time of life. We asked her if she was meeting someone for lunch and she said no, so we asked her to join us." This young woman, who was thirty-one, wound up joining their group as a Pink Hatter and making some very dear new friends. She became particularly close to a member in her nineties and they began talking several times a week and having dinner together once a week. When the young woman moved into a furnished apartment, the Queen City Red Hats all brought her care packages. When she moved back to Washington, she took her pink hat and lavender garb with her. She is now planning her wedding and has invited the Queen City Red Hats to attend. Guess what colors they are planning to wear?

A letter from Canada told us about some activities in Barrie, a small community north of Toronto, Ontario. Lynn Clark is the vice mother of Barrie's Butterflies, a chapter originally started by Jane Baier. Jane had recently moved north from Florida. The chapter's first gathering was at a restaurant called the Purple Pig. "None of us took offense at the name!" wrote Lynn. "Eighteen women showed up in purple and red outfits, and we made the front page of the local newspaper that weekend. This started a week of phone calls and inquiries, and from that article we have yielded eight new chapters and over 220 new members." Way to go, Butterflies!

"Though it sounds absurd, it is true to say I felt younger at sixty than I felt at twenty."
—*Ellen Glasgow*

Dottie Winkelman's parents spend winters in Texas, far away from their Michigan home. Dottie was concerned that her mom was missing her friends, and so she decided to do something about it. "As the Red Hat Honeys [near Fond du Lac, Wisconsin] 'Publicity Princess,' I knew the kinship of the sisters. Within two days, I had five chapters in towns near her who had extended invitations to my mother. One queen mother even sent her photo and phone numbers and said, 'Have your mother call me and we can ride to the luncheon together.' I was overwhelmed by the warm response. It was remarkable—perfect strangers acting like old friends." Dottie gave her mother all of the information, then checked in again a week later. Her mother said that the towns were too far away. Dottie tried to reason with her, but her mother was insistent. "Her answer shocked me," says Dottie. "She said, 'No, I don't think going that far away would work out. I decided just to start my own chapter here in the park.' And so a new chapter was born. She became friends with more than twenty ladies she had seen at the park's pool, in the laundry room, or in the recreation hall. My mother, the queen, has made many new friends right in her own neighbor- hood." Dottie doesn't have to worry about her mom, Ferne Hillman, being lonely any- more now that she is the queen of the Cit- rus Red Hats in Edinburg, Texas.

In Adelaide, South Australia, Colleen Jane Atkinson is the queen of the Red Hat Dames Down Under. As a child and teenager, she told us, her parents moved frequently, making it impossible for her to keep any longtime friends. She married young and developed a close friendship with her sister- in-law, a bond she cherished. That relation- ship lapsed after Colleen's divorce, but has since resumed. Deciding that she needed to extend her circle of female friends, Colleen went in search of a Red Hat Society chap- ter. When she couldn't find one in her area, she started her own. This led to con- tact with many women in South Australia.

"Within a few days of registering my chapter, I had an inquiry from a lady in South Australia. We are keeping in touch via E-mail and she is starting her own chapter. What an amazing disorganization the Red Hat Society is! I feel this is going to be a GREAT beginning and another joyful chapter in my life, another way to connect with the sisterhood of women whom I love and cherish so much. Life really does begin at fifty, sixty, seventy, and eighty if we so choose."

The Middle Age Crazy McDonough Mamas of McDonough, Georgia, got their start when Co-Queen Jennifer Roberts was going through a difficult period in her life. She lost her husband, who was forty-five, to a sudden heart attack, and in that split second, she says, "my life changed forever. I was in shock." When her daughter went away to college soon after, she had a tough time adjusting. She cried in her car on the way to work in the morning and on the way home in the evening, looking for any excuse to avoid going back to her empty house. When she read about the Red Hat Society, she wanted to join, but she couldn't find any chapters in her area that were accepting new members.

"Finally," writes Jennifer, "one evening when I was looking at the Web site again, I decided in a leap of faith just to do it." She registered a chapter, even though she wondered "how in the world I would find some ladies who wanted to come out and play with me." Six months later, there are thirty-two official members in her chapter and six more on the roster, ready to join at the next luncheon. "I seem to have something going on all the time now with my new friends. Now my daughter is home from school for the summer, and she said, 'Mom, do you think you can stay home one night?' I think back to last year, when I was suffering emotionally, and marvel at how, through the most tragic thing ever to happen to me, I found this terrific group of new friends, who all are a blessing to me."

When Queen Mother Diva Shirley A. Franklin of the Little Miracles of Flint, Michigan, was forty-six, she had a massive heart attack. Because her mother had died at the age of forty-one from a similar attack, Shirley was terrified. Although she survived, over the years she had two more heart attacks and was eventually told that she needed surgery. After having quadruple-bypass surgery, she began to feel better and do some church work. She thought about how she could make more women happy, and she chose to start a Red Hat Society chapter. "It took my mind off myself and showed me how great life is sharing stories with your 'sisters,'" she says. "After I survived what the doctors said I couldn't, my daughter began to call me 'Little Miracle.' And guess what? That is where the name of our chapter comes from. Because each day that God wakes us up, it is His miracle."

After the passing of Joanne Johnson's husband, a classmate she had seen at a recent high school reunion sent her a clipping about the Red Hat Society, along with a note saying, "Here is a project for you: Start your own chapter." It took a little while, but two years later, she finally did it. "In February 2004, nine friends and I had lunch and chose the name Cats in the Hats in Annapolis, Maryland, for our chapter. People started leaving messages for me, saying, 'We understand that you are queen of Annapolis.' I haven't decided whether to ask

Annapolis's mayor, Ellen Moyer, to join us or to move over and make way for the queen!"

CONNECTION JUNCTION

With the Internet at our red-gloved fingertips, we are making connections with women who live hundreds or even thousands of miles away! Eddy Gourley of the Crimson Chapeaus in Hemet, California, says, "Four years ago, at the age of eighty-two, my husband and I finally relented and invested in our first computer. Now I realize how the computer and being a member of the Red Hat Society have brought a new dimension to my life. Two years ago, I went on eBay and purchased a hand-decorated Red Hat Society tote from Lianne Paschette, a member of the Glitzgals in Melbourne, Florida. This was the beginning of a fulfilling friendship. We write E-mails weekly and find that we have many things in common. We are both cancer survivors. We are both Red Hatters. Despite the difference in our ages, we share many hobbies, like quilting and sewing. We share pictures of our grandchildren and our new great-grandchildren. A year ago, I was in Florida with my husband and we were able to meet and have lunch with Lianne and her husband. My life has been truly enriched through the Crimson Chapeaus in our retirement village. Without the Red Hat Society, Lianne and I would never have met!" The Red Hat Society planted the seed, but Eddy and Lianne nurtured it, allowing it to bloom.

Merle Neill tapped into the benefits of the Red Hat Society to ease her into a move she was planning. Merle was a member of the Special Friends chapter in Lubbock, Texas, and while she was considering moving to Louisiana to be near her daughter, she wasn't sure how she really felt about leaving her home and friends behind. "After making a trip to see the house and select paint, carpet, and tile, I returned home, put my house on the market, and began to make plans to move. But then reality set in: What was I thinking? How could I leave my home and friends, church, study club, and my beloved Red Hat Society sisters?" Merle's daughter did some research on Red Hat Society chapters in the area, and Merle was soon playing happily with the Red River Hatters in Shreveport, Louisiana. "I made great new friends and did things that were much different from the things I had done on the plains of Texas," said Merle, who has also maintained her membership in her original chapter and always enjoys hearing news from its members.

Sharing our lives with one or two people can lead to unexpected benefits. The story of Duchess Saundra Rae D'Arcy of the Cherokee Village Ozark Scarlett Women in Arkansas proves it. When she posted news on the Queen Mother Board on our Web site about a new man she had met, she soon discovered that the particulars of her developing romance were met with avid interest by many other Red Hatters, who then began to follow her postings. Her tale of their meeting, the development of their friendship, and his eventual proposal were shared as time went by. (Ever the soul of discretion, Saundra Rae never identified her suitor by his real name. She wanted to leave the poor man some privacy!) Thousands of red-hatted sisters all over the world eventually thrilled to the story of the couple's wedding. Real life is so much better than fiction, don't you think?

Even when you're overseas, the Red Hat

Society can often provide you with friendly faces in every port. Queen Mother Bev Fussell of the Dinki Di Divas in Perth, Western Australia, came to the United States with Lorna, the "Duchess of Doolittle," after spending five weeks in the United Kingdom. They called this leg of their trip "Red Hatting Across America" because of the warm welcome they received at all of their destinations. "We have been overwhelmed by the warm and generous offers of hosting it has been our good fortune to receive from some of our Red Hat Sisters," says Bev. Maryland; Washington, D.C.; New York City; St. Louis; San Francisco; and Los Angeles were only some of the stops on their Red Hat tour. They attended the Red Hat Society Big Apple Birthday Bash in New York and even managed to stop by our Hatquarters in Southern California, on their way to Los Angeles to catch their flight back to Australia!

 "The cure for boredom is curiosity. There is no cure for curiosity."
—*Dorothy Parker*

Our regalia makes it so easy to recognize our Red Hat sisters, even when a convention is over and we're waiting for the flight home. Donna Madrid, queen mother of the Red Queens, Chatsworth, California, was at the Nashville airport with her friend Lynn Tursky after the 2003 national convention. They were heading toward the gate when they heard people calling out to them. There, in the middle of the bar, was a huge table with twenty Red Hatters sharing a last few minutes of togetherness. Donna says, "We never, as you know, ran out of things to say to one another. We were never strangers. We just walked up and started talking. What a good-time group we all are! None of us knew one another, but there was a camaraderie. We all felt a bond, and we took it home with us. Do you suppose there is magic in our red hats?"

One non–Red Hatter who was stirred by our magic is Debra Yeska, a nontraditional Briar Cliff University student who was taking a course called "The Social Aspects of Aging." Debra chose the Red Hat Society as her subject for a presentation to the class and invited two local members from the Sioux City Crimson Glorys, Queen Renee Beacom and "Music Mama" Mary Chapman, to visit her class. Debra says, "They arrived dressed in full regalia and surprised and charmed my classmates. The sisterhood and joy of life permeated the room." Debra notes that her instructor has often emphasized the need women have for friends. Renee and Mary provided a perfect show-and-tell demonstration of the joy of that female companionship.

Interchapter relations are our specialty! Perhaps the United Nations should visit some of our gatherings and take notes. Barbara Best, a member of the Irresistables of Harbor Isles, Florida, got in touch with another Red Hat Society chapter, Silly Daze of Northport, and the two chapters organized a luncheon together. In order to encourage the making of new friendships, they shuffled chapter members so that each woman would be sitting next to someone she didn't know. This is such a good idea, because it is so easy to drive to a chapter event with a close friend, sit next to her the whole time, and ride home with her, too, never having made new acquaintances. How about trying something like this at your chapter event in order to ease one another (ever so slightly) out of your comfort zones? Why must we allow the boundaries of our lives to shrink?

"There are some things you can't share without ending up liking each other."
—*J. K. Rowling*

Wearing the red hat can help us to discard the stereotypes in our minds and make us recognize how much we have in common with those we may have originally perceived as being very different from us. Queen mother Jane Aldridge (La Bonne Vie, Steubenville, Ohio) wrote to tell us that her chapter has been blessed with a very diverse group of women. "Soon after our group was organized, I grew to truly appreciate one special lady, who was always there smiling. When someone mentioned that Sister Pauline would be coming one evening, I was amazed that we would attract a Catholic nun into the fold. Then I was told that she'd been coming all along and really enjoyed the sisterhood. I couldn't recall having ever seen a nun entering the party room, as I imagined a lady in a black habit sweeping in through the doorway. I kept a lookout for her but didn't see her, although I saw my cheery, smiling friend enter in a quilted hat covered in flowers. A woman walked up to her and said, 'Hello, Sister Pauline.' As I'd always pictured nuns to be stern-faced, ruler-cracking women in black, I was amazed to discover the sister within the Red Hat lady. She is unique and fun-loving, and my view of Catholic sisterhood has changed forever."

MaryAnn Raemisch, "Grand Duchess," (the Dazzlin' Darlin's of Dane County, Middleton, Wisconsin) found herself missing her chapter quite a lot while she was spending the winter in Branson, Missouri. She checked the Red Hat Society Web site for local chapters and contacted them, pleading "Red Hat withdrawal." She is thrilled that she did, since several chapters got in touch with her. She attended a luncheon and dinners, went to a play, saw a Branson show, and even modeled in a fashion show. Now she is a member of a chapter in Branson as well as in Middleton, and she'll never have to suffer those pesky Red Hat withdrawal symptoms again!

Another member who participates in activities with multiple chapters is Linda Shultz, queen mother of the Red Hat Jezebels in Brentwood, Tennessee. "I live in the Nashville area where there is always something going on at all times. It can be a busy life. But we also own two thousand acres in Iowa, and when we get there, I have nothing to do," writes Linda. "That is, until Sue Ellen started this wonderful group of ladies. There are four chapters near my farm, and I have met some wonderful women. Because of the Red Hat Society, I now have new friends and something to do while my husband is walking the fields. I can't tell you what this organization has meant to me. I met one of my father's teachers and a distant cousin of my mother's. Everywhere we travel, I take my purple and red—you never know when you might meet another Red Hatter!"

Diana Nunez, a member of Those Darling Red Hat Divas from Joliet, Illinois, was in Texas for her sister's fiftieth wedding anniversary. While she was there, she attended a luncheon with the ladies from the Chile Pepper Red Hatters in San Antonio, Texas, and took her niece with her. Sylvia, the queen mom of the Chile Pepper Red Hatters, is a wonderful hostess, Diana tells us, and Diana and her niece spent a very nice day with some of the members of that chapter. On their way home, Diana's niece asked her how long she had known these women. "I just met them today," Diana told her. "Isn't it wonderful to know that among the Red Hatters, there are no strangers, only new friends!"

"Personality can open doors, but only character can keep them open."
—*Elmer G. Letterman*

Serena Toro agrees wholeheartedly. She lives in Washington, D.C., and is the queen mother of the MarValous Red Hatters. When she got an E-mail from a Red Hatter in California who was going to be in town, she immediately invited her to a function they were organizing. Unfortunately, the timing was off and the woman wasn't able to meet her, but another member of the out-of-towner's chapter, also traveling, attended the gathering and she and Serena became friends. "She and her husband came to our family seder on Passover," said Serena, "and we got together again for dinner before she and her husband returned to California. I believe I have met a new good friend. Red Hatters are a great bunch of ladies!"

Queen Madam Lori Lane of the Red Hat

District in Bartlett, Illinois, has a son who lives in the Minneapolis area. While visiting him there, she went on-line and got in touch with a few ladies who lived in the area. None of them had ever met before, yet they met for tea at noon, began chatting, and didn't rise from the table until five P.M.! Lori says, "They called me 'visiting royalty'! What a hoot!" When she was home again, she also had the opportunity to answer an E-mail from a Red Hatter visiting her area. The two of them met for tea at the Drake Hotel, and of course Lori told the visitor that she'd be immediately recognizable, as she'd be the one in the Red Hat!

Another Red Hatter who is beyond tickled about the proliferation of our chapters is Bobbi Daugherty, queen of the Crone Jewels of Red Bank in Red Bank, New Jersey. She married a man who gets transferred every few years, so she is always trying to find a place to fit in, make new friends, and make connections. She finds that it gets harder as you get older: People are less open to forming new friendships, and you don't meet people through your young children, as you don't have any anymore. She related a negative experience she had when she tried to make a new friend at a pottery class. Bobbi had suggested that they get together outside of class. The woman's response: "No, I don't think so. I don't need any new friends." An experience like this could probably dampen anyone's enthusiasm, couldn't it? But Bobbi was undeterred, and when she discovered the Red Hat Society, she started a chapter. Now she has more than fifty new friends. Says Bobbi, "No matter where we are sent next, I know I will have all the friends I can handle and a place where I belong. I love it! I think this may be the best, happiest time of my life."

Karen Ise, queen of Le Chapeaux Rouge de Conejo of Westlake Village, California, agrees. Her version of retirement planning includes having lots of friends. "There has been a lot said about baby boomers," she wrote, "but after all the self-help books and psychological talk shows that are associated with our generation, one thing that we should know by now is that our happiness is our own responsibility. My friends and I often chuckle, as time marches on, about what we will do when we reach the retirement stage of our lives. I see my mother, alone at eighty-four, without family nearby and without friendships. She never considered that friendship is as important a factor as any other part of retirement planning. I don't fear the aging process. Although we are never certain what health or financial burdens may be ahead of us, I know that wherever I end up, there will be a group of wonderful ladies I can get to know and get to call my friends. All I will need is my red hat and an open heart."

A young wife sat on a sofa on a hot, humid day, drinking iced tea and visiting with her mother. As they talked about life, about marriage, about the responsibilities of life and the obligations of adulthood, the mother clinked the ice cubes in her glass thoughtfully and turned a clear, sober glance on her daughter.

"Don't forget your girlfriends," she advised, swirling the tea leaves to the bottom of her glass. "They'll be more important as you get older. No matter how much you love your husband, no matter how much you love the children you'll have, you are still going to need girlfriends. Remember to go places with them now and then; do things with them. And remember that girlfriends are not only your friends but your sisters, your daughters, and others' relatives, too. You'll need other women. Women always do."

What a funny piece of advice, the young woman thought. Haven't I just gotten married? Haven't I just joined the couple world? I'm now a married woman, for goodness sake, a grown-up, not a young girl who needs girlfriends. Surely my husband and the family we'll start will be all I need to make my life worthwhile!

But she listened to her mother; she kept contact with her girlfriends and made more each year. As the years tumbled by, one after another, she gradually came to understand that her mom really knew what she was talking about. As time and nature work their changes and their mysteries upon a woman, girlfriends are the mainstays of her life. After fifty years of living in this world, here is what I've learned:

Time passes.

Life happens.

Distance separates.
Children grow up.
Love waxes and wanes.
Hearts break.
Careers end.
Jobs come and go.
Parents die.
Colleagues forget favors.
Men don't call when they say they will.

But girlfriends are there, no matter how much time and how many miles are between you. A girlfriend is never farther away than needing her can reach.

When you have to walk that lonesome valley, and you have to walk it for yourself, your girlfriends will be on the valley's rim, cheering you on, praying for you, pulling for you, intervening on your behalf, and waiting with open arms at the valley's end. Sometimes, they will even break the rules and walk beside you. Or come in and carry you out.

When we began this adventure called womanhoood, we had no idea of the incredible joys and sorrows that lay ahead. Nor did we know how much we would need each other. Every day, we need each other still.

—Author unknown, found on the Internet

Linda Nargie, "Queen Mum of Fun," (the Hat Pack, Santa Barbara, California) put it beautifully when she wrote, "We can have a never-ending conversation. One subject leads to another. We feel one another's moods, joys, needs, loneliness, happiness, sorrow, and pain. As we grow older, I think this becomes even more evident. I believe the friendships we make now are even stronger than when we were young, for now they are to be trusted, cherished, and loved. We know they are here to stay."

"When I turned sixty, I took it hard," wrote Rosalie Rinehart of the McArthur Monday Marvelous Matrons, McArthur, Ohio. "I volunteer a lot, and I know that I can give and give and give, but then sometimes I have this empty feeling, as if I've given myself away. I was aware of a lot of wonderful women in the community, and some of them also seemed to be overextended. I was looking for companionship and I had heard about the Red Hat Society—it seemed like such a neat organization. For the last year, we have had so much fun and shared so much laughter. It's wonderful to be philanthropic, but sometimes it's also okay for me to take care of me and just have fun." This is exactly what I've been saying all along. Rosalie just said it better.

Red Hats encourage renewal of friendship and the beginnings of beautiful new relationships. We help one another get through the tough times by focusing on the good times—a dose of laughter and love can be stronger than any prescription written in a doctor's indecipherable handwriting. Miriam Cina joined the Red Hat Society as a gift to herself. She got divorced after nearly twenty-seven years of a difficult marriage, then found herself a job. When she lost her job, joining the Red Hat Society was her way of encouraging herself. And she's not the only one.

"I looked in awe at the gorgeous red hat my best friend was holding out to me," says Lynna Belin, a member of the Fabulous Founders in Fullerton, California. "Little did I know that this would bring with it a community of fun-loving, intelligent, and beautiful women. Not many years before, my life had taken a wrong turn due to black ice, an eighteen-wheeler, and a Ford Explorer. After rolling three and a half times into a deep ravine on a winter night, I found myself alive but a quadriplegic. I knew my God had been watching over me, and I began the long fight back to a meaningful life. Before being lifted from a smashed SUV, I was a graduate student, an RN, and a university teacher, among other things. In the intervening years, my best friend has done everything she can to get me back into the teaching community, and we have spent wonderful times on the telephone and just hanging out. Today I'm so thankful for the gift she gave me by opening the door to the Red Hat Society. These women are truly becoming my sisters and I look forward to many happy years together." All of us Fabulous Founders have enjoyed getting to know Lynna, thanks to her longtime friend (and mine) Maureen Burton. She has given as much as she has received. The blessings of Red Hatting go both ways.

"Nobody sees a flower—really—it is so small it takes time, like to have a friend takes time."
—*Georgia O'Keeffe*

The aforementioned Queen Linda Nargie met a shy woman at work, to whom she took a liking. So she did what any of us would do: She invited her to attend a Red Hat Society meeting. "Of course she was hooked," says Linda. "She took the title 'Queen of Love,' and I later understood why. She had survived two brain tumors, losing four years of her life in the process. During those years, she had to relearn how to eat, walk and talk." Linda visited this woman's home one day and was saddened to see the way this struggling woman was living. "Things were falling apart. A few of our members and their husbands joined forces and we transformed her little house into a home. She calls it her 'Doll House' now. Little by little, this person emerged from her shell and blossomed into someone outgoing and unafraid. I thank her for being such an inspiration in my life and to every-one who has come to know this amazing, wonderful woman." I would venture to say that this Red Hatter is very thankful for the day she met Linda. Queens like Linda make all of us look good!

Celebrating with friends and loved ones is certainly the cat's pajamas—but having friends stick with us when we're under the weather is definitely the cat's meow. Trudy Booz (the Ruby Circle, Lehigh Valley, Pennsylvania) took a serious fall at the Dallas convention, knocking herself unconscious in the hot tub. She didn't regain consciousness until she was at the hospital, and when she opened her eyes, Queen Toni Hoffman was holding her hand. "I didn't even know my name, much less where I was or how old I was," says Trudy. "As I started to regain my memory, I realized that Toni would miss the formal dance if she stayed much longer. I begged her to go, but she would not budge. When I awoke again, the former queen, Roberta Alessi, and Joan Turner, 'Princess Sunshine' were there, too. All three stayed with me until it was time to go back to the hotel. All the Red Hatters hovered over me with love and care, and when I got home, I was showered with cards from our group and from others—people I had never met—who had heard about what happened. Although I came home hurting all over and had to have six weeks of physical therapy, I felt very blessed to have such dear friends, and all because we met in the Red Hat Society."

Marge Tamblingson, queen of the Chapeau Rouge of the Great Lakes, Port Washington, Wisconsin, told us about a party they had for a member who was undergoing chemotherapy for breast cancer. Her hair was beginning to fall out, so they scheduled a hair-cutting party for her. Kay was seated on the backyard deck and her chapterettes took turns with the scissors, with a beautician neatening up along the way. Then they put her new wig on her head and surprised her by trooping out of the house with rubber bald-head caps and giving her a bunch of gifts, like hats, scarves, and visors. Kay truly knew that they all loved her and would be there for her no matter what. They pray that she will make a full recovery. Marge writes, "It turned what could have been a miserable time into a fun, lighthearted event with a minimum of tears. It is that magical Red Hat sisterhood that makes things like this possible."

When Jean Scott turned sixty, she was

feeling kind of lonely. She and her husband had few friends in the area, so she looked up her old school friends. One woman with whom she got in touch invited her to a Red Hat luncheon. "I had such a good time," said Jean. "They wanted me to join, but it was a bit too far to drive. So I went home and looked on-line, and sure enough there were several chapters here in Hemet, California. Now that I've joined the Good Time Gals, it has been such fun. Everyone is so nice. They make me feel welcome, and I no longer feel so alone."

Like many other siblings, Queen Linda Arends of the Florida Belles in New Port Richey and her sister Carol were not close when they were young. "In 1991," says Linda, "my husband was told that he had brain cancer. Two years later, Carol and her husband were visiting with us, when he went into a coma. For eleven days and nights, she never left me alone. Together, we took care of my husband, talked, and really got to know each other for the first time. At that time, we didn't know that six months later I'd be in Colorado, holding her hand at her husband's funeral. Now we both live in Florida and I like to say that we are sisters twice, once by birth and a second time because we are both Red Hatters and enjoying life as best friends!"

Eveline Wright Branan, vice mother of the Red Hat Mamas in Coshocton, Ohio, wrote in to offer her validation of our official slogan, "Red Hatters Matter!" She says, "I used to think that was just a cute term we used. I'm finding the longer I'm part of this wonderful group, the more I come to appreciate what it stands for. It's like when one wakes up or gets out of one's comfort zone and suddenly sees the world in a different way. Our group had only been together for about a year, when three of our members lost loved ones. We were there for one another throughout, and we decided to attend the funerals in full regalia. We donned our purple dresses and sat together in the church pew, putting our red hats on when it was time to walk up and say our good-byes to our sister's husband. It brought a smile in the midst of despair. I've come to realize that no matter where you live, where you are, if you are within reach of a Red Hat Society group, you are among friends, sharing sisterhood, help, and camaraderie."

THEN AND NOW

There are special qualities of peace and understanding in longtime friendships. The Sizzling Scarlet Sisters of Fargo/Moorhead, North Dakota, have only four members, according to June deWerff, and they've decided to keep it that way. They have been friends for fifty years, having attended grade school and high school together in Warren, Minnesota. Their greatest get-together, June says, was at the home of Ann and her husband, who have a "beautiful lake home on Flag Island on Lake of the Woods. Gwen, Doris, and I left early one morning for the five-hour drive north. It took us eight hours because we kept finding fun things to do on the way. We stopped for lunch in our hometown and visited garage sales and a quilt store. When Ann met us, we had a boat ride over to the island. We hung curtains, made jewelry, ate well, stayed up late, and went for nature walks. Ann showed us a bald eagle nest and later we saw the majestic bird fly over. It was the most wonderful slumber party we'd ever had." This is certainly testament to old pals, good times, and the incredible refreshment that a couple of days with old friends can provide.

Members of the Brookwoods Red Hat Society in Houston, Texas, have been hanging out for years and years. "There was a time over fifty years ago when the word *old* was not even a part of our vocabulary. As young wives and mothers, we came together by chance in a newly developed area," wrote Melba Holberg. "One by one, we came, built homes, started families, organized civic clubs, garden clubs, scout troops, schools, churches, PTAs, and parties. Always searching for ways to get together, we formed a coffee club, with the main purpose of just having fun and sharing neighborhood happenings. We shared in each new baby, in each child's starting school, in every birthday, graduation, and music and dance recital. This closeness was passed down to our children, and sometimes they were not sure which house was home. To announce these get-togethers, one only had to hang a red flag in front of the house and everyone would know where to go that morning or afternoon for the latest news and recreation. Gradually, over the years, many adults and children have gone, leaving a small remnant

Circle of Friends

When I was little, I used to believe in the concept of one best friend, and then I started to become a woman. And I realized that:

One friend is best when you're going through things with your man.

One friend is for when you're going through things with your momma.

Another is for when you want to shop, share, heal, hurt, joke, or just be.

One friend will say, "Let's pray together." Another, "Let's cry together."

One, "Let's fight together." Another, "Let's walk away together."

One friend will meet your spiritual need, another your shoe fetish, another your love for movies. Another will be with you in your season of confusion. Another will be your clarifier.

Whatever their assignment in your life, whatever the occasion, whatever the day, wherever you need them to meet you with their gym shoes on or to hold you back from making a complete fool of yourself . . . those are your best friends.

Men are wonderful, husbands are
excellent, boyfriends are awesome,
male friends are priceless . . . but if
you've ever had a real good girlfriend,
then you know there's nothing like her!
—*Author unknown, found on the
Internet*

of the original young mothers, who are now
hanging out red hats for an excuse to get together for the same reasons."

The Red Hat Society has helped to rekin-
dle more than one special relationship from
years past. Geri Wrobleski and Helen Latouske were pleased to share one such
story. Geri is a member of three Red Hat Society chapters in Illinois. One of these, the
Purple Dollies of Downers Grove, has
around 236 members. With such a formidable roster, it can be tough to keep track of all
the women, so the queen prepared directo-
ries to help members know more about one
another and to find others within the chapter
who had similar interests. Geri, who is seventy-two years old, was looking through the
roster when she spied a familiar name. Geri

dialed her number. "I said, 'Is this Helen Latouske from Westchester?' When I told her who I was, she gave a scream," Geri told us. "We were friends as newlyweds, when I was just eighteen and my husband, Mike, was in Korea. We lost contact with each other over the years, and it turned out that we had already been at the same gathering and not even known it. We were across the aisle from each other. It had been fifty years since we had talked—that's a half century of lost friendship." This is the kind of incredible connection we love to hear about. And it is happens surprisingly often!

At their fiftieth high school reunion, a group of old friends from Sweetwater Union High School decided to bring back their high school clique under the umbrella of the Red Hat Society. Edna Monk, the "Queen of Tarts," and her chapter, the Sweet-tarts, live in San Diego, California, and some of their members have been friends since grade school.

One revitalized connection, aided by Red Hatters, occurred between a mother and her estranged daughter. Vice Mother Kay Anderson was riding with several other members of the Red Hat Merrymakers, a chapter located in Bahama, North Carolina, on an outing to a Waukenabo Township, about an hour and half distant. On the way, she shared the sad story of the two painful years it had been since she had seen or heard from her daughter, from whom she was painfully estranged. When they arrived at their destination, they shopped and had lunch. As always happens, they enjoyed a lot of attention from the townsfolk. As Kaye walked with her friends, she heard a voice calling, "Nice hats, ladies!" Thinking (hoping) she recognized the voice, she turned around and anxiously searched the faces in the crowd. The young woman who had spoken saw her and cried, "Mom!" A tearful reunion followed. The rest of the chapter was teary also. Kaye says, "If it weren't for our red hats, the fate that took us to that town at that very time, the reunion would never have happened. Thanks, Red Hatters!"

 "It's the friends you can call up at four a.m. that matter."
—*Marlene Dietrich*

Marge Williams and Elaine Embrey are twin sisters, and " 'Tween Mothers" of the

Prominently Purple Red Hatters in Bay City/ Essexville, Michigan. They and their friend Dee Burnell were nursery mates in March 1944 in the Newborn Nursery of Michigan Bay's City General Hospital, and their mothers were roommates after they gave birth to them. "Elaine and I became reacquainted with Dee on our first day of nursing school in 1962," wrote Marge. "We have been close friends ever since." Dee has lived in Louisiana for the past thirty-seven years, and they always try to get together when she is in Michigan. The last time, they had a slumber party. According to Marge, they managed to get a few hours of sleep after hours of conversation, and then spent the next afternoon together, wearing red and purple, as Red Hat sisters. They lunched and antiqued in their red and purple—and then discovered that the car had a flat. Not willing to allow such a mundane inconvenience to interfere with their good time, the ladies had AAA dispatch a gentleman to handle the tire while they continued their shopping and beautifying. "We had our picture taken with the man who fixed our tire," says Marge. "He said that he felt like a celebrity when we told him that we'd like his photo. What a riot! Then we enjoyed virgin strawberry daiquiris and some french-fried ice cream, since Red Hatters are allowed to begin with dessert and then skip the rest of the meal if they choose to do so."

A Letter from One Red Hatter to Another

Dear Judy,

I just have to tell you, if I can find the words, just how much you changed my day. Let me tell you why.

I started the day by losing the keys to my car and had to drive our old beater— hardly runs, bad brakes, you get the picture. I was going to get a gift for my Michael, and when I got there, they had no more. Then I got a ticket for an out-of-date tag on the car I never drive. When I got to the Laundromat, I put the load in, then realized I had no cash. When I went to put the groceries and the wash into the car, it wouldn't start. My mechanic wasn't working and I had to find a tow truck. There was no one to give me a ride home, so I walked for forty-five minutes until I connected with someone via my cell phone.

By the time I reached my house, I was in tears. And there, hanging on the doorknob, was a small bag with a note saying "From one Red Hatter to another" and the most adorable little ornament—the very one I loved at the Christmas party—with the biggest, goofiest smile on its face. I just sat right down there on the driveway and cried.

For me, my dear Judy, this is what friendship, Red Hatters, and the Christmas spirit is all about. And for that wonderful and timely gesture, I thank you from the bottom of my heart.

> *Terri*
> *Sent from Terri Cash to*
> *Judy Duncan*
> *Red Hot Flashes,*
> *Greenville, South Carolina*

I don't think I can say it any better than that! This is what the Red Hat Society is all about.

6

The Consorts

An archaeologist is the best husband any woman can have: the older she gets, the more interested he is in her.
—Agatha Christie

You can't appreciate home till you've left it, money till it's spent, your wife till she's joined a woman's club. . . .
—O. Henry

What would we do without our significant others? We women are said to value relationships above all else; most of us would declare that to be a valid assessment. A successful marriage is a terrific source of support for both spouses. Some of us have had, or perhaps are still in, such relationships. But many women have learned the hard way that trust can be misplaced and that promises are not always forever. Whether we married the first young man we kissed or are making a second (or third) attempt to craft a successful marriage, whether we're learning how to pick up the pieces and refashion them into new and healthy relationships or are grieving for beloved spouses who have passed away, we'll all be able to relate to the stories that follow. Textbooks say that you need three things to survive: air, water, and shelter. I'd like to add a fourth: love.

NO BOYS ALLOWED

It has been interesting and gratifying to observe men's reactions to the Red Hat Society phenomenon. Initially, many of them expressed amusement and even a bit of befuddlement, unable to understand what all the fuss was about.

When our fledgling movement was just beginning to catch on, Sherry Friend, one of my own chapterettes, confided that her husband thought it was "stupid." Larry may dispute that now, but he does admit that he didn't really get it at all. That changed when he joined the crowd to watch a large contingent of Red Hatters (including several of us from the founding chapter) participate in the Doo Dah Parade. Here in Southern California, the Doo Dah Parade is a goofy spoof of the annual Rose Bowl Parade. That particular year, it included a group of folks wearing big cartons, painted to look like houses—running and jumping along the parade route to simulate a good old Southern California earthquake. There was also a large group of seventies-attired people (bell-bottoms, bushy sideburns, etc.) disco-dancing in synchronization. And then there was the Red Hat Society, its members in various rather over-the-top regalia. Larry had to admit that that was a great day, and he was disappointed when we didn't get around to participating the following year. I think he gets it now!

Over time, a great many men have begun to gain some insight into the mystery of the Red Hat Society, understanding how much this has meant to their wives and significant others. They've realized that their women are benefiting from their membership in this disorganization, actually lightening up and

enjoying life more. And a shrewd man real-
izes that a happier woman in his life leads to
a happier life for him, as well!

 "Every man who really loves his
mother, wife, or daughter is behind
you 100 percent."
—*From an E-mail sent by Jim
Hoover*

Such men can't help but observe the new
aspect of their wive's personalities, which
perhaps is emerging for the first time. It isn't
long before some of them begin wondering
aloud why there is nothing quite like this for
men. I have been asked this question quite
often as I travel and speak with husbands
and reporters. The most poignant incident
occurred in Atlanta, where I was told by the
husband of Diane Kuykendall of the Stone
Mountain Village Hatters of Georgia that he
should be allowed to join us. He had recently been the recipient of a heart trans-
plant and a woman's heart now beats within
his chest. Would this qualify him for membership? he wondered. I doubt that he was
entirely serious, but it was a sweet moment
nonetheless. The bottom line remains: The

Red Hat Society is, purely and simply, a "girl thing." It's not so much that men are excluded, as the fact they are just not qualified. They don't get the girl thing. And the truth is, they wouldn't want to if they could. They love doing their "guy things." Vive la difference!

But, that being established, it is important to note, as we always do, that we thoroughly appreciate the wholehearted support men offer us and the vicarious charge many of them get out of sending their wives out to play with their friends. Well, most of the time anyway.

Nancy M. Hasse's chapter, the Happy Hatters, Gainesville, Florida, had driven quite a long way to Mount Dora to attend a huge antique extravaganza. While they were strolling along, looking at the lovely pieces, a man came out from behind his booth and remarked, "My wife is one of you. She puts on that red hat and purple dress and goes out the door . . . and I never know if she is coming back or not!" Surely that was said with a smile! He probably knew that she was coming back in a good mood—but not until recess was over.

A group of couples in Florida enjoy going

out to lunch together after weekly Bible study. Not realizing that the Red Hat Society is indeed a girl thing, they originally attempted to register their chapter under the name of the R.O.M.E.O.S and J.U.L.I.E.T.S. The R.O.M.E.O. designation stood for "retired old men eating out," and the J.U.L.I.E.T. stood for "jubilant unabashed ladies intently eating together."

When they learned of the problem this presented, they changed their registration to just the J.U.L.I.E.T.S. of Panama Beach. However, the men still make great consorts and, occasionally at least, excellent chauffeurs!

As a woman of faith, I have been somewhat disheartened to discover that women who take their religious faiths seriously sometimes have even more trouble than others allowing themselves to come out to play with the Red Hat Society. In their attempt to obediently serve God, they may become so serious and rigid in their determination to be selfless that they have trouble taking a bit of playtime for themselves. I cannot speak for all faiths, but I know that the Bible has a great deal to say about the value of taking a rest from work and seeking refreshment for the soul—not to mention a real appreciation for laughter and celebration. So it has been extremely heartening to receive significant amounts of unsolicited support from male pastors. Many have taken the time to let us know of their wholehearted support of the Red Hat Society as a valuable recess for female members of their flocks. Have we heard from female ministers? We certainly have. They support the Red Hat Society by joining themselves!

It did my heart good to hear from "Hattie Red Hat" (aka Mary Helen Fry), the queen mum of the Cultured Pearls in Crawfordsville, Indiana. One of her fellow members, Betsy Strain (aka Lillibet Parsimonious), is a minister's wife. Both Lillibet and her husband encourage all the ladies to wear their red hats to church on Pentecost. The minister once announced that any women interested in adding a little more fun to their lives should contact the women in the congregation who "just happened to be wearing beautiful red hats."

"Lord Bill Fetch and Carry" is the husband and "Red Hat Gofer" of Maryanne Whatley, queen mother of the Red Hatters of Rincon, Georgia. He got his royal name at the convention in Dallas, bestowed by Queen Mother Linda Glenn (the Rowdy Red Hat Mamas of Northwest Wisconsin, Luck, Wisconsin) when she heard how loyal he is to Maryanne's Red Hat causes. He sometimes accompanies his wife to conventions (where he does his own thing while she attends Red Hat Society events). He has also been known to get up in the wee hours of the morning and chauffeur his wife and her chapterettes to a distant city to see *Menopause the Musical.* This kind of good-natured support is endearing—and appreciated.

We received a note from a gentleman named Jim Davis, who had heard about us and checked out our Web site. "What a fun and upbeat society you have created! My own hat, a sweat-stained green baseball hat, is off to all of you. I hope you will continue to inspire the rest of us to enjoy the whimsical in life, search for the common threads that bind us, and color our lives with fun and friendship. Though a male, I count myself as an honorable FORHS, or Friend of the Red Hat Society." Here's another testament that the Red Hat Society brings out

the best in people and encourages sharing—regardless of their sex.

The men we love support us when we're
down, sometimes in very thoughtful and
original ways. When one Red Hatter in Florida was diagnosed with a serious illness,
her husband decided to give her a good
reason to overcome it. He bought her a new
motorcycle to practice her balance on. "And
I shall ride it wearing a red hat under my helmet," she says.

"I love being married. It's so great
to find that one special person you
want to annoy for the rest of your
life."
—*Rita Rudner*

Judy Bloss, queen of the Vintage Gals in
Alachua, Florida, has a husband with a
great sense of humor. Judy's friend Nancy
Hasse, herself a queen (Happy Hatters,
Gainesville, Florida) tells us that Judy's hus-
band checks the caller ID on their phone.
Whenever he recognizes the number of a
Red Hatter, he answers the phone with a
cheerful voice, saying, "Red Hat Looney

Bin!" or "The Queen is Red Hatting; this is the answering service." The ladies really enjoy this guy!

When the Red Hat Gang of Purple Persuasion, a chapter located in Avenel, New Jersey, was brand-new, they gathered at Queen Joan Pochek's home to make jazzy red hats to wear for their first outing. "Rhinestones, sequins, ribbons, baubles, beads, tulle, and red cowboy hats were all over the room," writes Joan. As they worked on making each hat unique, she told the group that she must have a very special scepter to go with hers. Joan's husband, who had obviously been eavesdropping, brought a bathroom plunger into the room, declaring, "Queenie, this is for when you are on the *throne!*" The chapterettes immediately began to decorate it. But "Lady KayLea," apparently of the opinion that this scepter would not do, showed up a week later with a new scepter for the queen—a golden plunger shaped like a nude woman. Not one to leave well enough alone, KayLea had embellished it with "jewels," tulle, and beads.

Another man who has no problem treat-

ing his wife like Red Hat royalty is the husband of Ann Carol Lemiszko, queen of the
Red Hat Dixie Belles in Auburndale, Florida.
Ann says that her husband has always
treated her like a queen, but he really
showed his sincerity when he surprised her
with a charter for her very own chapter of
the Red Hat Society as a Mother's Day gift!
He obviously knew that the person who
charters a chapter (or receives one as a gift)
automatically becomes that chapter's
queen. Ann says that this shows his respect
for her, as well as his respect for all women.
And I'd like to point out that there isn't a
woman alive who wouldn't appreciate this
kind of treatment! I often say that our husbands cannot be kings, as a king would automatically outrank a queen, which would
create royal problems within households,
don't you think? But this guy certainly qual-
ifies as a prince!

Janet Dyer of Just Us Girls, Bloomington,
Illinois, has an RHS-friendly husband who
surprised her and her chapter when the girls
were out having dessert. He showed up to
join them, wearing a purple sweatshirt and a
red hat. Janet says, "He sat down with us

and then left the bill for me!" After he left, another man approached their table to ask how he could join, commenting that "it looked like so much fun." He must have been disappointed when he learned their chapter's name was Just Us Girls and that Janet's husband had been only a guest!

The guys just want in on the action, don't they? (And isn't it great that they feel that way?) Betty Orick of the Sassy Scarlettes of Apple Valley, California, says that her husband and his buddy, both retired U.S. Navy master chiefs, get a kick out of the "Red Hat thing." The guys came home one day from a "man shopping spree" and called to her from the garage. When she responded, she saw them standing there, laughing hysterically, with red satin baseball caps on their heads. They had bought ten caps for themselves and their friends and explained their intention of calling the group they were starting the High Desert Horny Toads. All that their buddies would be required to do in order to join was wear their caps, hang out in the garage, drink some beers, and tell old sea stories. Now, there are some guys who are being inspired to do their own thing. It sounds like they are already entertaining themselves. And more power to them!

One Red Hat Society husband, Andy Smith, was inspired to found a group he calls the Hard Hat Brotherhood. "This idea came to me after my wife became the queen of her own chapter," writes Andy, or "His Royal Highness Prince AnnWoo of Humor and Goofiness." (Char Smith is the queen of the Flaming Red Divine Divas in Dexter, Michigan.) "There was nothing more boring than dropping off my significant other at a Red Hat Society event while I was stuck on the outside looking in." He formed the Hard Hat Brotherhood so all husbands could "get together and do what we do best—guy things. Or, as my wife the queen says, 'belching, fishing, eating fried food, and watching sports on the big-screen TV.'" He told his wife that since he is now the "Head Hard Hat," she could be the "Hard Hat Hattress." She says, "Like being a 'Divine Queen Diva' was not enough!" The last we heard from Andy, he was busily accumulating chapters (crews). It will be entertaining to see how this group develops.

LOVE THAT LASTS

 "What is a husband? He is the one who, with a touch, can bring back the starlight and glow of years long ago. At least he hopes he can— don't disappoint him."
—*Alan Beck*

Statistics for marriage these days paint a glum picture. So it's especially heartening to hear stories of marriages that really last all the way from the paper anniversary to the diamond anniversary. And they *do* exist. The following stories prove one glorious thing: Romance is alive and well, at least according to some Red Hatters!

Donna Weaver of the East End Red Hatters in Lancaster, South Carolina, sent an E-mail to Hatquarters to tell us about the gift their chapter queen received from her "main squeeze" of fifty-four years. Queen Mary Moose did not expect anything earth-shattering from her husband, Buck, since he usually gave her a card with money enclosed so she could get what she liked. But she was flabbergasted by the gift he gave her for her seventy-second birthday. He casually asked her what in the world she had hit with her car. She rushed to the garage, expecting to see a damaged bumper, but instead she found the front door on each side of the car bearing big red-and-purple magnetic signs with the Red Hat Society logo smack in the center of each. Across the top, each sign read QUEEN MOOSE, and below the logo was EAST END RED HATTERS. Donna, aka "Princess Yum Yum," says, "This was the best birthday present ever. How do I know? Queen Mother Mary Moose is still smiling from ear to ear as she drives around this small southern Red Hat Society–infiltrated town." What a guy!

More proof that romance is alive and well out there came from Queen Carole Riddle of the Rouge Chapeau Tootsies in Hampstead, Maryland. As Carole's twenty-fifth anniversary approached, her husband suggested that they renew their wedding vows in front of their immediate family. Touched, she agreed, not knowing that he had secretly made plans to include a large group of friends, as well. For the occasion, he presented Carole with a beautiful beaded off-white gown and provided a dress for their daughter and tuxedos for their sons. The whole family drove to the chapel together, where Carole was stunned to see an entire congregation gathered. After the ceremony, they enjoyed a full-blown reception. Carole says, "One son walked me down the aisle. Our oldest son was best man, and our daughter was my bridesmaid. This is one anniversary that I will remember and cherish for the rest of my life." Wouldn't we all?

Romance can be more subtle in its expression, though just as genuine. Mary Ann Bronson, queen mother of the Forever Young chapter in Jackson Gap, Alabama, says that her eight children do not think their dad is a very romantic kind of person, but she knows better. "We have been married for fifty-one years and he still holds doors open for me, makes sure the car is filled with gas and has the tires checked if I drive the car for any distance, always kisses me when he leaves the house for any reason, helps with the housecleaning when guests are expected, and is most supportive of the Red Hat chapter I started. He also delivered our seventh child in an army hos-

pital elevator in Germany . . . but that is another story." (I, for one, would love to hear
this story!)

Mary Ann says she was disappointed
when her husband didn't support her idea
of throwing a party to celebrate their tenth
wedding anniversary (they were stationed in
Munich at the time). But on the day itself, as
they were on their way to dinner, he stopped
at a jewelry store and said, "Pick the ring
you would have chosen ten years ago."
There had been little money for a nice ring
when they first married. Mary Ann asked
Dick, "When did you think of doing this?"
His answer: "Ten years ago." Beautiful!

Red Hatter Margaret Morlan of the Scarlet Swans in Ocala, Florida, wrote to tell us
about her happy reunion with her high
school sweetheart—forty-four years after
graduation. She and her first boyfriend had
gone their separate ways after high school,
married other people, and raised families. In
1990, both now single, they began to exchange letters, eventually reconnected, and
were married in 1992. "It is still hard to believe at times, " says Margaret, "but you
never forget your first love."

"There is always some madness in love. But there is also always some reason in madness."
—*Friedrich Nietzsche*

More than thirty-two years ago, a chance glance at a high school yearbook led a former classmate of Betsy Sprenkle of the Nipomo Nifties, Nipomo, California, to look her up. He had gone to Cleveland, Ohio, to visit his mother, who was ill, and took the time to visit some of his old classmates. They chided him for missing their twenty-fifth reunion and showed him photos from that reunion of the class of 1944. When he asked if any of his classmates lived near him in his new home in Los Angeles, he discovered that one former classmate did—Betsy! Not only did she live in L.A.; she lived only a few houses away from him—on the same block! When he got home, he got in touch with her, and when he discovered that she was divorced, he asked her out to dinner. "Ten weeks later," says Betsy, "we were married."

Husbands and significant others are not the only men who have come alongside us and shown kindhearted support. Among the many examples of this was a ninetieth birthday party thrown by the Red Hots of Austin, Texas. According to Queen Jean Zurow, the honoree, Nellie Murphy, was given several gifts containing ninety items: ninety pieces of candy, ninety jokes, et cetera. Since the cake had ninety candles on it, the local fire station sent over nine firemen to put them out safely. The birthday girl spent the time flirting with the firemen, and a good time was had by all. (These firemen were logical guests for a second reason: They were wearing red hats even before we were!)

The Winston Red Hatters of St. Petersburg, Florida, were dining at a local restaurant when the waiters began pouring champagne for all thirty-five members. They were very surprised, as they hadn't ordered it. The waiter explained that a gentleman at the bar had ordered glasses of the bubbly for them. Queen Mother Jane Perry went over to thank him, and he commented that the ladies deserved champagne because they were spreading such happiness.

The Razzle Dazzle Dolls of St. Louis, Missouri, experienced even more generosity. Queen LeAnn Hurford says, on Valentine's Day, "Eighteen beautifully purple-and-red-dressed ladies had high tea at the Adam's Mark Hotel, where they were enjoying themselves immensely with gales of laughter and great conversation." When they asked for their bill, they were informed that a gentleman who had watched them had already paid it! Since we all wear red, and Valentine's Day is about love, Red Hat Society members have a special place in their hearts for Valentine's Day already. But this sure made one chapter's Valentine's Day more special!

Yes, even very brief encounters with anonymous men can be the cause of warm feelings. "Queen Bee," Alberta Patch-Slegaitis of the Go Go Girls of Durham, North Carolina, was moved to write this poem, which demonstrates what I'm talking about:

Red Hat Episode
A little Red Hat woman in a red hat
  and purple gown

*On her way from a Red Hat dinner to
   an appointment across town
Stopped to ask directions at a
   convenience mart
And was greeted by the manager,
   pushing a loaded cart.
"May I help you?"*

*She asked for the directions. He
   obligingly replied,
"Straight ahead to light, one mile. On
   the right-hand side."
Then, looking directly at her, with
   admiration in his eyes,
He made another comment, which
   took her by surprise.
"You are a pretty woman. God bless."*

*To a lady in her eighties such words
   are seldom said.
Back straight and walking taller, red
   hat on lifted head,
She left the store in regal style and
   went upon her way.
Perhaps unknown to him, the young
   man had made her day.
The echoed words still linger, "Pretty
   woman."*

The Red Hat Society has been referred to as "the second women's movement." The primary woman's movement would no doubt be the feminists' push for equality a few decades ago. It may be that some Red Hatters have reaped benefits from the advances made by ardent feminists, at least careerwise. But if we are indeed the second woman's movement, it seems to me that it is important to emphasize one significant difference between the first and second movements. We Red Hatters are not angry with men, nor is there any stridency in our attitude toward them. We recognize that male-female relationships continue to be, as they have always been, complicated and wildly variable. But in general, we are very glad to have men in our lives; we are interested in relating with men with mutual goodwill and support. We love them.

BUT sometimes we just must do our occasional girl thing!

7

The Nature of Nurture

"Working mother" is a misnomer. . . . It implies that any mother without a definite career is lolling around eating bon-bons, reading novels, and watching soap operas.

—Liz Smith

Sometimes the laughter in mothering is the recognition of the ironies and absurdities. Sometimes, though, it's just pure, unthinking delight.

—Barbara Schapiro

Few things are more satisfying than seeing your own children have teenagers of their own.

—Doug Larson

PARENTING

Our beloved children and grandchildren have been responsible for a very high percentage of the lines on our faces. The years spent rearing children brought countless experiences of joy and sorrow. The grandchildren who are coming along seem to be taking up right where their parents left off.

Years ago, I saw a quote somewhere, which I have remembered—perhaps not word for word, but sufficiently to paraphrase it: "Children are people who pass through our lives and disappear into adults." They do, don't they? We have all spent bittersweet hours poring over family photos from years gone by and have experienced pangs of loss mingled with warm feelings of nostalgia. Where did those little children go? We remember the sounds of their piping voices, even the smell of their little round cheeks, warm from their naps, and the sensation of holding their small hands. But those children no longer exist, except in photos and our memories. The adults they have become remain dear to us, but the precious infants, toddlers, and teenagers they once were are not reclaimable.

Ah, but we still have our precious memories, don't we? And some of the most amusing of those memories can still provide us with fodder for storytelling. A lot of us Red Hatters did not yet know one another when our children were small. But now we can haul out some of those old stories, dust them off, and share them with new friends. In the process, we get to enjoy them all over again.

OUT OF THE MOUTHS OF BABES

 "Lions and tigers and bears! Oh my!"
—*Judy Garland, in* The Wizard of Oz

If there's anything that children love, it's animals—unless those animals are scary! Sue Prohaska, the queen of Skyline's Classy Ladies, Omaha, Nebraska, recalls driving through Safari Park with her children when they were still quite young. The trail was covered with signs informing visitors about the animals they were likely to see as they drove. Occasionally, some of the friendly creatures would come right up to the cars and attempt to poke their heads through the windows to say hello.

"My youngest, Justin, was just learning to read," Susan told us. "He yelled to his dad to stop and not go any farther. 'The sign says "Little Killer Animals Ahead!" ' he said." Upon examination by the adults, what did the sign really say? LITTER KILLS ANIMALS.

We have all had experiences involving misunderstandings between ourselves and our children. Sometimes they are humorous; sometimes they are touching. Linda Heusinkveld, aka "Queen Spend-a-Buck," of the Royal Glitzy Chicks in Lansing, Michigan, shared this story: "One late-spring morning, the sun came streaming into the kitchen window, warming the two-inch-tall marigold stem sitting on the sill. My four-year-old son, Aaron, had planted a seed in a paper cup one day as part of a Sunday school lesson. He faithfully watered it, and he was elated when green actually popped up through the soil. We had started mixing up a batch of cookie dough, and as we measured and added the eggs, butter, and sugar, I talked Aaron through the cookie-making process. With my back to my son, I said, 'Now it's time to put in the flour.' When I looked at him, I saw him standing there holding the cup with his marigold seedling, his eyes brimming with tears at the thought of sacrificing his flower for the cookies. Needless to say, we *both* learned a lesson that day."

"The most important thing she'd learned over the years was that there was no way to be a perfect mother and a million ways to be a good one."
—*Jill Churchill*

Linda C. Brady sent us a story she called "Who's Your Daddy?": "While stationed in Okinawa, Japan, my husband was sent on temporary duty to Vietnam. My daughter was only two years old at the time. She was used to running to him when he came home from work in his uniform, but now only I came through the door in the evenings. She missed him very much. He had only been gone a couple of weeks when we stopped at the base cleaners to pick up some things. The door behind us opened and in walked an officer in uniform. My daughter took one look and started hollering at the top of her lungs, 'Daddy, Daddy.' The officer looked at us with a very surprised facial expression and said, 'Oh no! I'm not responsible.' I couldn't help but burst out laughing. The poor officer's face was brick red."

Sandra Olmsted of the Aqua Babes of Northern Kentucky, located in Erlanger, Kentucky, wrote that when her daughter was young, she asked a lot of questions. When she asked her daddy something he couldn't answer, he would make something up, not wanting to disappoint his little girl. Whenever the child asked Sandra a question for which she had no answer, she would say she didn't know, then suggest that they find the answer together, perhaps by looking it up somewhere. This policy of honesty backfired in an unexpected way. One day, her daughter said, "Mom, how come Dad is so smart and you don't know anything?"

I'm sure that we all agree that honesty is the best policy. But is it okay to finessse the truth to get what we want? The late K. C. O'Connor of Fayetteville, North Carolina, wrote about her effort to outwit a child she encountered at a toy store at the mall. She and the little girl both zeroed in on a purple feather boa hanging in a wall display in a store. KC swore she almost fainted with delight when she saw it, but in order to prevail, she had to convince the little girl that she really did look better in the pink one. Triumphantly heading out to her next Red Hat Society meeting in her regalia, complete with new purple boa, she was amused to hear her daughter say, "You look like Barney in drag. I wouldn't be caught dead in a purple boa. If you go out of the house looking like that, please don't tell anyone your name." KC laughed all the way to the car. "So here I am at my first meeting," she related, "my boa around my neck and the room full of other purple dinosaurs. They asked me what I wanted to be called. The only appropriate answer was, 'Barney'!"

Children view us through their own eyes. To them, we have always been, and will always be, "Mom." And we may discover that they see us very differently from the way we see ourselves. Karen Foster of the Renaissance Red Hats in San Diego, California, sent us a story about a special Christmas gift she received from her fifteen-year-old son one Christmas. "As Christmas neared, his excitement began to build. He handed me a box and said, 'Open this first! I was walking past a store window and saw this, and I thought, That's my mom!' Imagine my surprise when I opened the box and pulled out a slinky black satin suit, complete with vest and a filmy white shirt. I was speechless. I was mortified! But the look of pride on Carl's face brought me out of it. 'You love it, don't you?' he asked. 'You can wear it on New Year's Eve. Try it on.' Well, I tried it on, and it fit perfectly. The problem was that I looked like a slinky cocktail waitress. He thought I looked beautiful. Yes, I wore it on New Year's Eve, and I wore it proudly. This was a gift from my son. I thought about what other people would think when they saw me dressed like that. But what did it matter? The look of joy on his face when I donned his handpicked outfit was the confirmation that I had made the right decision."

 "Human beings are the only creatures that allow their children to come back home."
—*Bill Cosby*

When Carolyn C. Donohoe (the Endorphin Divas, Allen, Texas) was a young single mom, she had a tough time financially. She sent this story about a time when her children were in first, second, and fourth grades. "One morning, I had to cut open our last tube of toothpaste so the children could brush their teeth," she told us. "We had no baking soda or anything else they could use. I had about a quarter in my purse and wasn't going to get paid until Friday. The children wouldn't buy it when I told them it would be okay to brush their teeth with just water for a few days. They were very upset, because it had been Tooth Week at school and they were afraid that 'Jack Black' was going to get their teeth. In exasperation, I finally told them (and not in a real gentle spirit, either) that they would just have to trust their teeth to God for a few days, as I had done all I could. With that, we left for work and school. When we got home in the evening, I opened the mailbox and discovered a sample tube of toothpaste. My eight-year-old son put his hands on his hips and said, 'Mom, did God bring the toothpaste by Himself, or did He send an angel?' My answer? 'God uses everyday people to do his work, sweetheart. Even you and me.'"

A MOTHER IS A MOTHER IS A MOTHER

The children who touch our lives are not always our own. Leone Bradfield (Divas by Design, Aurora, Colorado) had a history of volunteering at her children's schools and working on their PTA boards. During the time her own sons were at the local high school, she helped to establish a tradition of holding a special farewell ceremony for graduating seniors. Even after her sons had graduated and gone on, she made a point of continuing to attend these ceremonies. Leone, aka "Queen Tussy Mussy Latte," says, "As the seniors, many weepy, passed by, one petite young woman came up to me and hugged me, saying, 'I knew you'd be here, Mrs. B.!' I was startled, but I finally recognized her as a young lady who had gone to elementary school with my son. After sharing a hug and congratulating her, I asked, 'Carly, why did you say that? Whatever made you think I would be here?' Her response overwhelmed me. 'I knew you would be here, Mrs. B., because you held the classroom door open for me on my first day of kindergarten. You were the first one to welcome us to school and tell us to have fun. It's only right that you're here to say goodbye.' Needless to say, I started to cry. Carly helped me see that all the meetings, all the baked cookies, all the late nights standing up for kids at school board meetings to try to improve things for them was worth every single minute."

If we keep our eyes open and watch for them, life often presents us with compensations, which can make up for earlier unmet needs. Dodie Frank, queen mum of the Scarlet O'Hatters of Santiago in the Villages, Florida, did not have a good relationship with her mother when she was growing up. "As I got older, it deteriorated even more. I prayed that God would give me a daughter; I had three sons, whom I love dearly, but no daughter." Eventually, though, one of Dodie's sons married a lovely woman named Michele, whose friendship and love Dodie appreciates deeply. Now Dodie has a granddaughter named Kayli, and the three of them often share wonderful girl times together. "Last year," wrote Dodie, "I took Kayli to a high tea with our Red Hat chapter. This year, both Michele and Kayli are going to the high tea, and they've had a grand time picking out their lavender dresses. Thanks to the Red Hat Society, I get to enjoy my two favorite girls even more."

The Virginia Vamps of Richmond, Virginia, were having a festive Christmas lunch at the Jefferson Hotel when two mothers came in with their two young daughters. Margie Nolan Cowles and the Vamps told them all about the Red Hat Society, and then the girls took pictures with the Red Hatters. "Imagine our surprise when, an hour later, the girls returned with their mothers to show us their new purchases. They decided they liked the Red Hat Society so much that they were going to start their own club. They purchased polka-dot hats and planned on starting their own Polka Dot Hat Club with their friends. Apparently, these little ladies had already figured out the value of having girlfriends."

A SPOONFUL OF SUGAR

How often we hear it said that we can experience life in new ways if we practice learning to see things through the eyes of a child. This simple exercise can provide us with whole new perspectives on life. Linda Ressler started the Southwestern YOYO's: Pink Divas and Scarlet Dames, located in Brighton, Illinois, partly because her daughter Michele wanted to be a Pink Hatter. When Michele was a baby, the pediatrician whom Linda chose for her daughter was a woman, as was the dental assistant who took care of Michele's teeth. Left without a baby-sitter one day, Linda took Michele with her on a visit to her own doctor. When he came into the room, Michele became alarmed. While Linda tried to chat with her physician, Michele tugged at her skirt for attention, her voice getting louder and louder. Asked what was wrong, Michele said very seriously, "Mommy, that's no doctor. That's just a man!" The doctor laughed and said that he'd never been put down so quickly by a female. Linda realized that Michele, having only been taken care of by professional women, didn't know that men were equal in the workplace! Indeed, when they got home, Michele ran inside, yelling, "Daddy, did you know that a *man* can be a doctor?"

Seeing through the eyes of a child is one thing, but believing everything they say can be a mistake. The queen mother of the Mysterious Red Hats in Des Plaines, Illinois, Terry Helwig, was hospitalized after being diagnosed with multiple sclerosis. Her mother, a Red Hatter in the chapter, took Terry's daughter Katie shopping to buy a robe, nightgown, and slippers for Terry to wear in the hospital. "While the clerk was ringing up the items," recounts Terry, "Katie told her that these were for her mommy, who was in the hospital with PMS."

As a middle school science teacher, Lucinda Denton of the Nonpareils, Knoxville, Tennessee, got to teach her class about human growth and reproduction. When they learned about the birth process, a student whose father was an obstetrician brought in pictures of newborn babies. As the girl finished sharing the photos, Lucinda thanked her and asked, "Where does your father practice?" "Oh, he doesn't practice," replied the girl. "He's a real doctor."

Beverly Furman of the Crone Jewels of Red Bank, New Jersey, heard a story from one of her clients that gave her a chuckle. The client's husband had been trying to clean their fish tank, but didn't get it quite right. One of the tropical fish died. Their four-year-old son wanted to know why it had happened, so his parents explained about heaven. When the child's grandmother passed away at the age of ninety-six, they told him that she had died. The little boy wondered aloud what she had been doing in the fish tank!

When Deb Furber, aka "Lady Lace," of the Raspberry Margaritas of Cambridge, Ontario, Canada, was living in England, her father passed away. To give her time to get home, the family delayed the funeral until the following Friday. Deb's nephew, Neil, was in second grade at the time. During a religion lesson at school, the teacher told the class that Neil's grandpa had died and was going to heaven. Neil piped up and said, "Not yet—not until Friday." Neil is now twenty years old, and this story still provides the family with much amusement.

Children may not understand the deeper aspects of life and death, but they are still capable of profound insights. Judy Joines is a member of the Keowee Key Red Hatters in Salem, South Carolina. She shared a story about something that took place when her twenty-five-year-old daughter, Lisa, was suffering from cancer. When Lisa's young cousin heard of her illness, she asked her mother if Lisa had a teddy bear with her. Her mother said that she wasn't sure, and the child said emphatically, "Nobody can be sick without a teddy bear!" Judy reports that the small cousin's family promptly sent a teddy bear to her daughter. "She dearly loved that bear and what it represented, and it stayed with her in the hospital even when all her human company was shooed out." This bear started a tradition that continues to this day. When an older male friend of Judy's entered the hospital, Judy sent him a bear, as well. The man appreciated the bear so much that he later delivered it to an even older friend of his when that friend was hospitalized. This patient had become deeply depressed, refusing to talk even to his doctors. A few days after giving the bear, the friend returned to the hospital for a visit. Judy passes on what happened: "When he entered the room, his friend was looking at him gleefully. The bear was hanging on top of the IV pole, and the patient would now talk to the medical staff, but only if they directed their questions to the bear. Everyone, including the patient, was filled with hilarity after only a few minutes in the room. We understand that the same bear later went to a very young tonsillectomy patient, with instructions to pass it along to someone else when it was no longer needed."

All of this because a small child was able to put a basic human need into words!

> "I must take issue with the term 'a mere child,' for it has been my invariable experience that the company of a mere child is infinitely preferable to that of a mere adult."
> —*Fran Lebowitz*

We Red Hatters love to let our "inner children" out to play. In doing so, we temporarily allow ourselves to shed some of the rigid dutifulness of the adult and let the innate enthusiasm and carefree attitude of childhood reemerge for a bit. What fun to experience an afternoon, an evening, or a week-end in a deliberate state of uncomplicated enjoyment of the moment! What joy to play with our friends in a spirit of generosity and caring. We may have to act grown-up—but not *all* the time.

GRANDPARENTING

 "The very fact that you don't look or act or feel like the grandparents of even a generation ago does not mean that you are less, but that you are more—in effect, an evolved form of grandparents, primed to do a bigger and more challenging job than any group before you."
—*Arthur Kornhaber*

 "Never have children, only grandchildren."
—*Gore Vidal*

When a young couple welcomes their first baby, they are thrust into a whole new role: They are now parents! But they are not the only ones who are called on to make a major mental adjustment: The parents *of* the new parents (we Red Hatters) must now learn to see *ourselves* in a whole new light: We are now grandparents! The power to affect everyone around them positively radiates from those tiny creatures who are holding court in their bassinettes. From the moment they arrive on the scene, they change *everything.*

Now, I can't speak from experience here, as I do not yet have grandchildren. But many of the members of the Fabulous Founders do, as do lots of other people I know. I have watched these friends be reduced to puddles of quivery jelly by these little beings, whether it is a first grandchild or a tenth grandchild. It seems that all the gentle jokes about grandparents are all too true: This baby their son or daughter has produced is so unbelievably exceptional that there can never have been such a baby born before in the history of the world. No more gorgeous, precocious creature could ever have lived. In its way, that perception is true. Every child really does present the world with something new when he or she enters the world—a talent, a personal quality, an element of change, a new beginning. There never actually *has* been a child quite like this one before. The new parents have great responsibility to care for and raise this new human being, whom they love more than they could have imagined. But the grandparents have all of the joy and little of the responsibility—they have somebody new to play with!

WHAT IS A GRANDMOTHER?

A grandmother is a lady who has no little children of her own. She likes other people's.

A grandfather is a man grandmother.

Grandmothers don't have to do anything except be there when we come to see them. They are so old, they shouldn't play hard or run. It is good if they drive us to the store and have lots of quarters for us.

When they take us for walks, they

slow down for things like pretty leaves and caterpillars.

They show us and talk to us about the color of the flowers and also why we shouldn't step on cracks.

They don't say "Hurry up."

Usually grandmothers are fat, but not too fat to tie your shoes.

They wear glasses and funny under-wear.

They can take their teeth and gums out.

Grandmothers don't have to be smart.

They have to answer questions like "Why isn't God married?" and "How come dogs chase cats?"

When they read to us, they don't skip. They don't mind if we ask for the same story over again.

Everybody should try to have a grandmother, especially if you don't have television, because they are the only ones who like to spend time with us.

They know we should have snack time before bedtime and they say

prayers with us every time, and kiss us even when we've acted bad.
Authors unknown, taken from papers written by a class of eight-year-olds, circulated on the Internet

Children and puppies go together like coffee and cream. But Queen Jo Simon of the Spring City Red Hatters in Waukesha, Wisconsin, says that her grandsons had not been able to have a puppy because their dad (Jo's son-in-law) was in the U.S. Army and the family didn't stay in one place for long. Eventually, Daddy left the military and the family settled in the Midwest. Kerri, Jo's daughter, located a dog with a litter of puppies in their new neighborhood and she took one home, planning to surprise her little boys with it when they got home from school. She put a note on the front door—"I am cute and cuddly and love to play. I want to come to your house to stay!"—and waited inside with the puppy on her lap. The boys came home, read and misunderstood the note, and rushed inside, yelling, "Grandma Simon's coming to live with us!" "Needless to say," says Grandma Simon, "my grandma heart overflowed with joy when the story was shared with me." The puppy? I'm willing to bet that it was an agreeable compensation!

Many times, little children have very generous impulses, but sometimes they need help to act on those impulses. Ruth Reisinger of Martin's Red Hat Girls in Baltimore, Maryland, shared a special Christmas story about her eight-year-old grandson, Alex. A month before Christmas, he and Ruth were looking through a catalog together. Ruth exclaimed over a photo of an adorable stuffed cat, remarking that she would just love to have one. Alex went directly home and let his parents know, insisting that they get that cat for Grandmom for Christmas. Wouldn't you know that that stuffed cat turned out to be *the* gift in huge demand that year? There wasn't a store or catalog that hadn't run out of that item. Ruth explained to Alex that she would be content to wait until later for one, but this wasn't good enough for Alex. He managed to come up with what he considered the perfect solution. He would ask Santa Claus for it, and when Santa left it under the tree, he would pass it on to Grandmom. When this plan reached Ruth's ears, she became determined to find a way to obtain one of those cats, then somehow see that Alex received it in time to "surprise" her with it for Christmas. She made several attempts to do that, once even rising at 4:30 A.M. to stand in line at a store. (Of course, the cats were sold out before she reached the head of that line.) Finally, she convinced a salesperson in one of the stores she frequented to call her if any of those cats suddenly became available. On December 23, she got the hoped-for call, rushed to pick up the cat, and delivered it surreptitiously to her son's house. On Christmas morning, she says, "Alex waited at the door for me to arrive. I will forever treasure the look on his face when I opened the box." Boy, the things a kid will go through to make his grandma happy!

Little girls love stories about other little girls—especially little girls who have glamorous adventures. Mary Vivian, queen of Talking Through Our Hats in Grand Haven, Michigan, has a granddaughter who was fascinated with Eloise (the character in the books by the same name) who lived at the oh-so-fancy Plaza Hotel. Mary had vacationed at the Grand Hotel on Mackinac Island in Michigan, and she thought a seven-year-old who dreamed of visiting such a place might enjoy a weekend at the Grand as a treat. "We took a carriage ride to the hotel and then walked up the long sidewalk. Logan's eyes were wide with excitement. Our rooms were bright red, pink, and lime, the Esther Williams pool had snow cones in many different flavors, and Logan danced for hours to the band in the ballroom. It was the perfect adventure, and one that neither Grammie nor Logan will forget."

A letter came from Sandy Brewer of the Boston Belles, a Massachusetts chapter, who says that her family has always been very demonstrative in showing their feelings for one another and that she has tried to instill this in her grandchildren. When her grandson Charlie was four, she went to his very first soccer game. "He was doing quite well scoring points," she says, "although it was for the opposite team. None of the children had ever played before. It so happened that I had to leave before the game was over. As I was walking back to my car, I heard the coach yelling, 'Murphy, where are you going?'" Sandy stopped and looked back, just in time to see little Charlie running after her, the soccer ball still in his hands. As he ran, he yelled to the coach, "I have to kiss my Nini good-bye. She's leaving!" I guess the devotion between grandparents and grandchildren goes both ways.

Queen Bonnie Harper of The Red Hats Are Coming! The Red Hats Are Coming! in Eau Claire, Wisconsin, owns a bar. "One busy Saturday," she writes, "on her way to do some shopping, my daughter stopped in with my three-year-old grandson, Dylan. He proceeded to go around the bar and tap every customer on the leg and state that the bartender was his grandma. One of the customers teasingly asked him if he was married, to which he replied, 'No, but if Grandma wasn't married to Grandpa, I'd marry her.' Even the tough men at the bar had a tear in their eyes at that tender response."

We Red Hatters are famous for our willingness to try new things, even when they do not come naturally. Ronnie Moore (Just 4 Fun, Havertown, Pennsylvania) was having her daughter teach her to use a computer and was finding it frustrating. Ronnie told her daughter that she felt like she couldn't do anything right. Her seven-year-old grandson, Jason, piped up, saying, "Yes you do. You know how to make your grandson happy." I guess that's something that goes both ways, too.

Sometimes it is possible to delight your grandchildren in unusual ways. Jean Bowley of Jean's Queens in Hawthorne, Florida, managed to do that. She relates that in 1997, she had a stroke on Christmas Eve. After several weeks in the hospital and lots of rehab, she was able to begin walking again. Shortly after that, Jean's daughter and her family came to visit. Jean's husband told the family to wait in the dining room. He wheeled Jean to just outside the dining room door and she pulled herself to her feet and walked into the room to surprise her family by showing them how far she had come. Squealing at the top of her lungs, her three-year-old granddaughter cried, "Look, everybody! They fixed her!"

THE LAST WORD

Little children haven't lived long enough yet to grasp all the nuances perceived by the adults in their lives. Marlene Casper's son teaches in an international school in Thailand. While visiting his family over the Christmas holiday, Marlene (the Red Hat Roses, St. Paul, Minnesota) found herself absorbed in reading directions while helping her five-year-old grandson, Sira, assemble a complex toy. While she was busily engaged in trying to fit bits and pieces together, Sira asked for her attention, wanting her to look at another gift he had just opened. "I'm putting this together; I can't look right now," said Marlene. "Well, Grandma," said Sira, "you have two eyes, don't you?"

The English language can be frustratingly inconsistent; it seems that there just aren't any hard-and-fast rules that don't have multiple exceptions. When they are small, some children run afoul of this truth. But they can be quite sophisticated, trying to apply rudimentary logic to this language they are learning, often with humorous results. When my son, Shane, was tiny, he learned that a froth of soap bubbles was referred to as "suds." Therefore, in his lexicon, a single tiny bubble was a "sud." Using the same logic, a single bruise was a "bru." Let me tell you, it was far easier to let him believe this than to try to explain the way this stuff worked.

Sometimes the humor comes from simply hearing something incorrectly.

Queen Mother Joey Lambert (Aged to Perfection, Orange, California) still laughs when she remembers the time her three-year-old granddaughter asked if they could mix up some "banana butt bread."

Another Red Hat gram who is still shaking with laughter at a grandchild's comment is Queen Mum Carol Jursik, of the Red Rovers of Akron, Ohio. "When my grandson was three years old," she tells us, "we were driving in the car, he in his seat in the back. I said to him, 'I'm going to have to take you to church.' He said, 'Why?' I replied, 'So you can learn about God.' 'I already know about God,' Dominic told me. After a few minutes, his voice piped up again. 'What I want to know is, who is God's wife?' Before I could respond, he answered his own question. 'Oh, I know,' he said. 'It's Mrs. God.'"

Lucinda Denton of the Nonpareils in Knoxville, Tennessee, has a young granddaughter named Madeline. One day when Madeline's mother had an early meeting, her dad decided to take her out to breakfast in a fancy restaurant. She was feeling quite grown-up and paid close attention as her father placed his order, and when the waitress asked what she would have, she confidently replied, "Eggs." The waitress then asked, "How would you like them?" Having never been asked this question before, Madeline replied, "Hatched."

Sometimes children find the actions of grown-ups befuddling. One Christmas season, Queen Mum Diane Frost (the Pine Island Chick-a-dees, St. James City, Florida) added holiday charm to her decor by removing the framed pictures from the walls of her home, wrapping them with gift paper and bows, and rehanging them. When her eight-year-old grandson, Brent, arrived to visit, he ran around the house with excitement and asked who the presents on the walls were for. Dee explained that underneath the fancy facades they were just the same pictures that had always hung there. Brent, looking perplexed, asked, "Aw, Grandee, who's gonna want your old pictures?"

Kathie Quisenberry (the Red Hat Mamas,

Marquette Heights, Illinois) was entering a store, holding the hand of her five-year-old granddaughter, Ashley, when Ashley announced that she wanted Kathie to teach her to crochet. Kathie told her that she would do that, but not until Ashley's hands grew a little bigger and stronger, so she would be able to hold the crochet hook correctly. Ashley, dismayed, exclaimed, "But Grammy, you have to teach me now, because you're almost dead!" "P.S.," wrote Kathie, "I had only just turned a healthy fifty."

Pauline Simone (the Calendar Girls of El Dorado Springs, Missouri) and her husband were baby-sitting for their three-year-old granddaughter, Simone, so they took her along when they attended the dog races at the Woodlands Track in Kansas City. Pauline explains: "Prior to one of the races, one of the dogs was taken out at the last moment. I commented to my husband that I had seen horses scratched from a race, but never a dog. I asked him why he thought it was scratched. The answer came not from my husband but from Simone, who said, 'Well, Grandma, probably he had an itchy.' "

Retarded Grandparents
(Retirement in the Eyes of a Child)

After Christmas, a teacher asked her young pupils how they spent their holidays away from school. One child wrote the following:

We always used to spend the holidays with Grandma and Grandpa. They used to live in a big brick house, but Grandpa got retarded and they moved to Arizona. Now they live in a tin box and have rocks painted green to look like grass. They ride around on their bicycles and wear name tags because they don't know who they are anymore. They go to a building called a wrecked center, but they must have got it fixed, because it is all okay now. They play games and do exercises there, but they don't do them very well. There is a swimming pool, too, but in it they all jump up and down with hats on while they talk to each other. I guess they don't know how to swim. At their gate, there is a dollhouse with a little old man sitting in it. He watches all day so nobody can escape. Sometimes they sneak out. They go cruising in their golf carts. Nobody there cooks; they just eat out. And they eat the same thing every night—early birds. Some of the people can't get out past the man in the dollhouse. The ones who do get out bring food back to the wrecked center and call it potluck. My grandma says I should work hard so I can be retarded someday, too. When I earn my retardment, I want to be the man in the dollhouse. Then I will let people out so they can visit their grandchildren.

—Author unknown, found on the Internet

Gerry Smart (Bella Luna Ladies, Tampa, Florida) shared that when her granddaughter, Francesca, was graduating from kindergarten, the microphone was passed around to each graduate so the kids could tell everyone what they wanted to be when they grew up. Various predictable answers were given, including doctor, nurse, lawyer, teacher. Francesca's stated ambition brought down the house. In an excited voice, she proclaimed, "I want to be a

Hooter's Girl!" Her parents probably crawled under their chairs.

One Red Hatter shared this: "As grandmother of nineteen grandkids, I thought I had already heard the best of stories—that is, until last week. I was taking care of my nine-year-old granddaughter when she brought up having periods, which she had just learned about from her mother. We had a long talk about it, and my two female dogs were sitting by my feet, so I explained to her that all female animals go through that. So she said, 'The dogs don't.' I then explained to her that I'd had the dogs spayed. She was quiet for a little while, and I was thinking to myself, Well, Gram, you still have it in you. But then my grandaughter looked me in the eye and said, 'I'll tell you one thing. I am either going to be spayed or fixed, whichever.' "

While we are discussing the birds and the bees, I'd like to share something my daughter, Andrea, said when she was small. (No, she doesn't qualify as a grandchild, but, as you may remember, I don't have any, and this story really fits here.) With a very intent expression on her face, she was watching Dolly Parton perform on television. She finally asked a question about Dolly's amazing physical attributes. I explained that while all adult women have breasts, these can vary in size quite a bit. Andrea cogitated on that for a moment, then commented, "When I grow up, I don't want really big ones, because they'd get in my way, but I don't want really little ones, either, because I wouldn't feel very feminine. I think I'll grow medium ones." I think a person with this sort of attitude is referred to as being "unclear on the concept."

Queen Evelyn Knight (the Diamonds in the Rough, Homosassa, Florida) has a granddaughter who is in her second year at Ohio State University. During a recent visit to her grandparents' home, the young girl observed Evelyn, who was all dolled up in her best purple-and-red finery, leaving for a Red Hat event. "Gram, I can't believe you go out in public dressed like that," she commented. Evelyn says, "There she stood in her baggy jeans and a shirt two sizes too large. I told her, 'I am senior enough to wear anything I please and get away with it, and you are young enough to do the same.' We both enjoyed a good laugh and a *big* hug."

That's just one more example of diffusing potential conflict with humor.

Queen Mother Gloria Kirkland of the Juliet Red Hatters, Mt. Juliet, Tennessee, shares a story that illustrates the generation gap between her and her grandchildren.

"My grandchildren were visiting, and I thought I'd show them some of my old things. When I showed them my high school typewriter, they said, 'Where's the monitor?' When I showed them my 45-speed record player, one of them asked to play a video. Another day, my granddaughter kept asking me to take her somewhere, and I told her she sounded like a broken record. She replied, 'What does *that* mean?'" Fortunately, Gloria has been able to just roll with this and keep her sense of humor.

JUNIOR RED HAT SOCIETY SUPPORTERS

A lot of us have caused embarrassment for our younger relatives the first time or two they saw us in our regalia. But as they have come to understand what our getups are all about and the spirit they represent, the embarrassment has turned to bemused pride. The grandchildren, in particular, have expressed encouragement for our silly adventures and support for our new determination to enjoy life.

Virginia Wingo, queen mother of the Kansas City Kids in metropolitan Kansas City, was shopping with her granddaughter on a visit to Texas when she spied a red hat she just loved. Unfortunately, it was already on the head of another shopper, who was obviously preparing to buy it. Virginia struck up a conversation with this woman and they soon discovered they were both members of Red Hat Society chapters. Virginia generously encouraged her sister Red Hatter to buy the hat, as it looked good on her. She swallowed her disappointment and began to peruse the jewelry counter. A few moments later her granddaughter, Jacquelyn, popped up with that same red hat, now on *her* head! She had followed the other shopper and convinced her to buy a different hat!

Helen Gonzalez is the queen mother of L.A.D.I.E.S. (Lovely, Ageless Dames in Excellent Shape), a chapter in Tampa, Florida. Aside from her own chapter she also social-izes with another group, composed of Red Hatters from Tampa and the adjoining towns of Odessa and Lutz. Helen and her friends Helen Beeler, Helen Meisner, and Linda Farkas took their granddaughters out to what they called a "Grand Teenie Tea." The girls, who all say they plan on being Red Hatters someday, attended in lavender outfits and pink hats. They had such a good time that the young princesses are already planning what to wear to the next Grand Teenie Tea. Funny how so many of these special occasions turn into ongoing rituals. When we have special times, we usually want to find a way to repeat them, don't we, no matter what our age!

A sweet tale came from Queen Mum Angela Byrne of the Jersey Tomatoes, Crawford, New Jersey, whose four-year-old granddaughter Gianna has been going on play dates since she was a baby. The child was at Angela's house as she dressed for an evening with her Red Hat Society ladies. She looked at her grandmother and said, "Are you going on a play date with your friends?" Angela says that she was closer to the truth than she knew!

"Anyone who uses the phrase 'easy as taking candy from a baby' has never tried taking candy from a baby."
—*Anonymous*

Queen Suzy Szymczak (the Red Hat Rovers in Huntsville, Alabama) has apparently discussed me, the "Exalted Queen Mother," with her little granddaughter, Brittany, at some point. Brittany was watching TV the day of the British Queen Mother's funeral. Suzy says she came into the kitchen and said to her, "Grandma, she *was* important. When you die, is your funeral going to be on TV, too?" She seemed relieved when Suzy told her that it was not me who had died, but merely Queen Elizabeth's mother.

Claudia Watkins, queen of the Red Hat Mommas in Sonora, California, lives about a hundred miles from her youngest grandson, TJ. When TJ was in kindergarten, Claudia volunteered to make the trek to spend a day with his class, helping with classroom assignments. Claudia says, "I was so excited! An idea hit me. I'll go as a Red Hat grandma! I dressed up in my purple outfit and favorite red hat and took along our new mascot, Rosey the Red Hat Bear, who has her own red hat, and a purple tutu besides. My grandson was thrilled to see me dressed up. He was so proud of me! It made him feel so special, and I can't tell you how wonderful I felt. This was one of the most precious moments in my lifetime. How blessed I am!"

The granddaughters of Queen Mum Judi Taylor are thirteen and five. The girls love watching Judi get dressed up in her beautiful red hats. And when they see how much fun their grandma is having, they want to play, too. Judi found a way to indulge their wishes by outfitting them as pink princesses and letting them ride on the Dazzling Dames (York, South Carolina) float in the annual St. Patrick's Day Parade. The little girls had a wonderful time practicing their queenly waves for all of the loyal subjects in the crowd. I predict that these three will be right there the next time the Dazzling Dames are in a parade.

While they may not express any interest in wearing regalia, some of our grandsons express their support in other ways. Gerry Petrich's grandson went on a trip to Cancún, Mexico, with his family. Not long after, Gerry received a package from him containing a crushable red hat. A note, tucked in by her grandson, read, "Hi, Grandma. I got you a present in Cancún. Mom was talking about the club you belong to with the red hats, so I found one for you to wear in the summer. . . . I couldn't find anything for Grandpa, but he can look at you when you wear this and see how beautiful you are. Love, Dave."

The venerable humorist Sam Levenson once said, "The reason grandparents and grandchildren get along so well is that they have a common enemy." Facetious though this remark was meant to be, at its core is an undeniable fact: Grandparents and their grandchildren have a special bond, quite different from that between parents and their own children. Grandparents have lived long enough to understand that it is okay to allow kids to be kids and to know that much of the behavior that gives parents fits will be outgrown. They may also have a lot more time to spend with these smaller people, time for sharing long walks or conversations, time to color or go to the movies. Ideally, they are better able to spend spells of unstructured time with the children.

Grandparents have already raised responsible adults; those responsible adults are now the parents of their grandchildren. The parents are the ones whose job it is to train and mold. The grandparents are then freed up to be their grandchildren's best buddies!

8

Mama Bear and Papa Bear

Parents are like shuttles on a loom. They join the threads of the past with threads of the future and leave their own bright patterns as they go.
—Fred Rogers

A mother is not a person to lean on but a person to make leaning unnecessary.
—Dorothy C. Fisher

Sooner or later we all quote our mothers.
—Bern Williams

As long as our parents are with us, we remain children in their eyes—even when we have become parents, and possibly grandparents, ourselves. The relationships we have with them bring deep joy and profound sadness, similar to those we have with our own children and grandchildren. When our parents are gone, they remain with us in our hearts and minds; their influence is indelibly etched in our memories, on our faces, and in our very beings, as well. Because of this, as we continue to grow older, we encounter situations that seem to be "happening again for the first time." Or, as Yogi Berra said, we experience "déjà vu all over again." Your mother's voice will echo in your head as you tell a child, "Be careful! Remember to call us when you get there," or you will be reminded of your father when you tell your children to keep their toys out of the driveway. Mom will pop into your head as you perform the same chores you saw her do so often. When your husband walks your daughter down the aisle, you will remember your own father doing that with you. The older we get, the more we are cognizant of the circle of life, the endless progression of generations, each one deeply influencing the next one.

We cannot begin to repay our parents for their love and care. Instead, our focus becomes our own children. By nurturing them, we pass along the gifts that we ourselves received from our parents. If we do this well, our parents will consider their jobs well done. And our own children will learn from our example, just like we learned from our parents.

A story I once read somewhere sticks in my mind. It concerned a Chinese household containing three generations—parents, children, and an elderly grandmother. The parents and children regularly ate their meals at a table together, but the grandmother was shunted aside to a separate small table and given only old battered dishes to eat from. After the grandmother's death, the parents were disposing of her things. Seeing them add the old dishes to the trash heap, the children objected loudly, saying, "Don't throw those away; we are saving them for you!" Ouch.

In gratitude and love, we will want to do all that we can to make our parents' later lives as enjoyable and fulfilling as we can. The same people who loved and supported us now need our help and care in a new way. Red Hatter Marie Haney (the Cats in the Hats, Ogden, Utah) wrote to tell us about a time when she was taking care of her elderly parents. She regularly drove 120 miles round-trip to spend time with them and help them perform their errands. "I always tried to take them on a picnic in the canyon to give them an outing, along with doing the shopping, cleaning, and laundry. One holiday weekend, we were looking in the canyon for a vacant table on which to have our lunch. Everything was taken. I finally found us a place near a couple who were reserving a few large tables for their group, and I assured them we would be out of the way before long. They sat back and watched as I helped my father, who had Parkinson's disease, and my mother, who was blind, to the tables, spread out the lunch, and helped them with their needs. We had a lovely time, and when I cleared the picnic away and was helping them back to my car, the couple walked over to me. 'We've been watching you,' they said, 'and we've decided we should start being nicer to our kids.'"

Brenda Kronberger's chapter, the Flambeau Red Hat Jewels in Park Falls, Wisconsin, helped her celebrate her father's eighty-ninth birthday, arriving at his nursing home after a luncheon with a band, ice cream, and cake. "My father just sat there and sang and smiled," she said. "The residents at the nursing home all just smiled. They loved the party. It was by far the best." It was such a suc- cess, she said, that they "can't wait to go back with the band for Christmas!"

When we inevitably lose a parent, sharing our feelings can help us to process our grief. Joan F. Ricks, queen mother of the Bo Peep Classy Ladies of Gainesville, Florida, was with her ninety-one-year-old father when he passed away. "Daddy's great- granddaughter was expecting her first child," wrote Joan. "Caitlin was born the same day that Daddy died. The pastor re- membered that when Daddy, who was the superintendent of the Sunday school, was asked about attendance, he would respond, 'Some are going and some are coming.' So he used that theme as his message and re- ferred to Daddy's passing and Caitlin being born. The church was decorated for Christ- mas and was so beautiful. When we walked out, snow was falling. What a glorious sight! I felt so clean, and I knew the Lord was with us."

Memories will always make our parents live again in our hearts. And sometimes an object, even a homely one, can tie us to parents we've lost. An old bundt pan, kept in her kitchen, causes Loretta DiGennaro of the Almondjoy Red Hat Society in Alexandria, Virginia, to reminisce about baking with her mother: "It was the bundt-cake pan," she says. "That damn pan made me stop in my tracks on an ordinary December morning in my kitchen. 'I'll will you this cake pan,' my mother used to say, kidding me. We would laugh together while making cakes for the upcoming holiday season—carrot cake, rum cake, ginger cake, and yogurt cake. My mom and I were a team, the two who baked for the family's enjoyment. While mixing ingredients, we would talk and share our thoughts—somewhat unusual behavior for a teenage girl and her mom. But the closeness lasted a lifetime. When I married and moved away, we would still get together for baking sessions. These days didn't last long enough. One afternoon in late summer, my mother called me with her bad news. Our world, our kitchen, our times together changed. Suddenly, we were involved with doctors and hospitals. Instead of finding new recipes to try, we were searching for information about radiation and chemotherapy. Meanwhile, the bundt pan sat idle, and my mother passed away. Recently, I found an envelope Mom had given me before her first operation. I hadn't opened it at the time. It was full of handwritten recipes, ones she knew by heart and had written down to share with the next generations. With the bundt-cake pan on the counter and recipes in hand, I decided to make the carrot cake. Over tea, I'll remember all the wonderful times spent in the kitchen with my mom. And I'll probably cry."

"You don't pay back your parents. You can't. The debt you owe them gets collected by your children, who hand it down in turn. It's a sort of entailment. Or if you don't have children of the body, it's left as a debt to your common humanity. Or to your God, if you possess or are possessed by one."
—*Lois McMaster Bujold*

Shirley Silvola, a member of the Bodacious Dames of Sunrise, Florida, wears a pair of her mother's old tennis shoes to Red Hat Society meetings. Shirley's mom had come to live with her when she was in the early stages of Alzheimer's. She had a mystical attachment to those shoes and insisted on wearing the ratty old sneakers to church for Easter. "She was so adamant about it," says Shirley, "that I stopped making it an issue. I told my friend Fanny the story and she came over and decorated them in purple and pink, adding sequins, glitter, and paint, and made them look so fancy. Every day, Mom would go and look at those shoes and say, 'How cute.' After she passed away, I kept meaning to get rid of those shoes, but I just never could do it. When Fanny called and said she had signed me up for the Red Hat Society, I opened the closet to find some purple clothing, and all I could see were those purple tennis shoes of Mother's with the purple sequins and flowers. As I put them on, I knew Mom was in heaven laughing her head off at her funny girl wearing her sneakers. They are twenty years old now, and I wear them to every meeting and event."

Donna Greenway, "Queen of Feathers" of the Rosie Red Hats in Wellington, Nevada, wanted to tell us how the Red Hat Society revived memories of her mother. Donna's mom was a flapper in the twenties, and Donna has kept her dress and feathered headband in a box under her bed for all of these years. After she joined the Red Hat Society, she began rummaging through her things, looking for decorations for her new red hat. "There was my mother's dress and feathers," she wrote. "My mother would have loved being a Red Hatter. She never met a person she did not like and was always helping everyone she knew. When I saw the ostrich feathers, I knew that Mom had to be a Red Hatter with me. Now all my many red hats have some of my mom's feathers on them. The burden of losing her is lessened when I know that she must be laughing and having a ball seeing me in my red and purple, with black feathers on my hat."

Sharing our Red Hat Society fun with our mothers who are still with us is an excellent way to nurture current relationships. "In the fall of 2002," writes Joy Breedlove, co-queen of the Dixie Belles, a chapter in

Blairsville, Georgia, "my parents moved away from the town and home in which they'd spent more than forty happy years and retired to the north Georgia mountains. They purchased a new home near the area where my children and I live. While they had wanted to make this move for ages, it was hard leaving friends and memories behind. At the same time, my friend Sandy and I decided to start a chapter of the Red Hat Society. When I shared this with my mother and told her that I had a red hat for her, her face lit up! She looked forward to each of our gatherings, but none more than that first one, where she was warmly greeted and made several new friends. Unfortunately, about a year later, she passed away. (Cards from Red Hatters decorated her hospital room while she was sick.) But the months she was able to be a Red Hatter gave her such pleasure. I am very thankful that we were able to share those experiences."

Mother-in-law jokes are ubiquitous. Most of us thought they were funny, until we became mothers-in-law ourselves. Now they probably make us wince a little, hoping that surely *our* daughters and sons-in-law don't hold negative opinions of us. (How could

that possibly happen?) Maybe finding ourselves in a new situation has caused us to
take a harder look at our own relationships
with our mothers-in-law and to reevaluate
our positions a little bit. Sometimes moth-
ers-in-laws form genuinely close relationships with the husbands or wives of their
children.

Founding Queen Mother Linda Suzanne
Rotterman, of the Classy Coastal Red Hat
Sorority, a chapter in the San Diego area of
California, formed a relationship with her
mother-in-law that was as dear as the one
with her own mother had been. Linda lost
her mother, Elaine, to cancer two years before she met the man she was going to
marry. "Along with Gene came a ready-
made mom and dad," she said. "I finally had
two parents again to love and cherish.
When my father-in-law became ill, I went to
Florida to help care for him. My mother-in-
law had a long journey ahead of her. I
watched this courageous lady spend all of
her time at the hospital and deal with the
challenges of handling things my father-in-
law had always taken care of. She never
complained once. We laughed and cried,
giving each other the support needed to

face what was ahead. And we did it. We even found time to buy a big red hat covered in little lights to wear to the hospital. He dubbed us 'The Red Light Ladies.' "

RoseMary Salzman, queen of the "Wild" Wild Rosies in Wild Rose, Wisconsin, and her father planted a special memory together before he passed away. "Memories are the glue that holds our thoughts of loving and caring together," writes RoseMary. "In September, my father turned ninety. This was a biggie! I wondered what I could do that would make this his most memorable birthday, both for him and for me. I thought about his life and what had been important to him over the years. My mind turned back to work-filled days each spring, when we would plant Christmas trees on his tree plantations. How I loved to work with my dad! It was there that I really learned about the man I loved so dearly. Finally his special day arrived. As he sat in the yard swing, I came around the house with a shovel and gloves and handed them to my father, saying, 'Dad, put these on—you're going to plant a Christmas tree!' Dad's eyes sparkled as he put on the gloves and began to dig. Soon everyone at the party was pitching in.

From the youngest to the oldest, we each had a chance to help. Six weeks after this magnificent day, my dad passed away after a stroke. This proud tree stands, its small branches reaching heavenward—a living sentinel on my lawn. As I sit in my swing and look at the tree, I think of Dad. He's here with me."

Imperial Queen Mum Kathy DiBona of the Hollywood Red Hot Hatters in South Florida says, "I am nearing sixty and my mom, Alice Drabick, is eighty-two. I crowned her this past year as our 'Grande Mammou,' and she looked so regal and proud! What a fabulous thing to be in a magical type of childhood once again, playing dress-up, with not a care in the world, having your own mother playing right alongside you all the while. After years of hard work, worrying and surviving, now we get to spend time having the time of our lives!" Kathy and her mom recently inducted Kathy's baby sister, Rosie Turner, now dubbed Baby Red.

Another such note came from Mary Willman, "Princess of Charms" of the Sassy Red Hatters in San Diego, California. "My sweet mother was welcomed into a chapter of Red Hatters in Santee, California, on her eighty-fourth birthday. They were so warm to her, and I would love to honor them the way they honored her. She had wanted to be a Red Hatter ever since my dad passed away three years earlier. She usually comes to visit each winter, and so we surprised her on her birthday at one of our Chocolate Parties. The queen, Suni Jordan, and her vice queen and sister, Lexi, were so dear . . . they introduced her as 'Queen Char from Afar' and presented her with a beautiful gift of chocolate and a red rose. She was thrilled, as her wish had been granted. I was reduated that very day, having turned fifty years old, and I'll never forget that day or the happiness it brought my precious 'Mum.' She has since returned to Minnesota and joined the Duluth Dames. Unfortunately, she missed the first meeting because she was admitted to the hospital with a case of shingles. True to her colors, she says they were definitely red and purple. The nurses in the ER marveled at the tiny little daisies she had painted on her toes. Just plain 'fun' has kept her young . . . and beautiful."

If we are fortunate enough to have one or both of our parents still living, we are keenly aware that this is a temporary situation. The quality of the time we spend with them now will strongly influence the depth of our regret when they are gone. The time to build happy memories with them is now, while we have them with us.

If they are already gone, our memories must be our comfort. Unfortunately, the memories that some of us carry are not happy ones. Although these memories cannot be eradicated or changed, it is still vitally important to make our peace with them. I have known several people who have not been able to put unpleasant memories of their parents' treatment of them behind them. The emotional burdens they bear and the havoc this wreaks in their lives can be hideously destructive and rob the future of its potential happiness. It seems to me that it is helpful to realize that, with very few exceptions, our parents did the best they could, just as we have done our best with our own children. Forgiveness and acceptance can allow us to move into the future without dragging heavy loads of anger and bitterness. There really can be great times ahead—especially when you've got your red hat on.

9

Woman's Best Friend

Animals are such agreeable friends—they ask no questions, they pass no criticisms.

—George Eliot

A dog is the only thing on earth that loves you more than he loves himself.

—Josh Billings

If there are no dogs in Heaven, then when I die I want to go where they went.

—Will Rogers

We use the word *love* in so many ways in our culture, and we all know that some of them are superficial. We can't compare the love we say we feel for french fries with the way that we love our children. When the word is used in its most serious sense, it conveys sincere, deep attachment. So maybe we don't love a lot of the things we say we do. But we *do* love our animals. No, they are not children, but the way we feel about them is certainly closer to the way we feel about our children than the way we feel about our fries, isn't it?

More than half of all American households contain pets of some kind; dogs and cats, of course, predominate. As in other areas that have meaning for us, we Red Hatters love to share stories about our animals. Some of our beloved pets shared our homes with us when our children were small; some are more recent arrivals. But they all hold a special place in our affections, and when they are gone, we grieve.

The value of strong relationships applies to the give-and-take we experience with our animals, because they possess and express their own personalities just as we humans do. Animals surely give as much—in most instances, more—than they receive from us. Our pets can sense our moods and empathize with us in beautiful ways. I have an acquaintance named Helen, who raises purebred Burmese cats, whom she refers to as "the kids." She told me about the day she lay face-down on her bed, crying over the sudden death of one of her all-time favorite cats. Another of the cats in her house was the mother of a new litter of kittens. This cat anxiously cir-cled Helen as she lay on her bed, showing obvious agitation. She abruptly jumped down from the bed and disappeared downstairs for a short time. Suddenly, she was back, holding one of her newborns in her jaws. She gently deposited the tiny creature right next to Helen's tear-swollen face, purred briefly, and then re-turned to the rest of her litter. This was an obvious gift of love. (Guess which cat be-came Helen's new favorite?)

My little canine companion, Frosty, is a huge part of my life. When I first brought him home, seven years ago, I had no prior experience of having a dog that was just mine. To say that we bonded would be a severe understatement. With few exceptions (at least when I am in town), Frosty goes where I go. He is so ferocious in his devotion that he keeps his little Raisinette eyes trained on me at all times, and he is never happier than when he is in my arms. My next-door neighbor likes to joke that when he dies, he wants to come back as my dog. Spoiled? Sure, but whom does it hurt?

Since I have had Frosty, my world has truly expanded. People stop me all the time to comment on how cute he is, or to ask about his breed. (His father was Maltese/ Lhasa apso; his mother was poodle/ Pomeranian. In my opinion, this makes him a Malti-poo-pom-apso!) These people also like to share stories about their dogs. Sometimes these preliminary comments lead to all sorts of fascinating interactions, which I would otherwise have missed. Overall, I believe that opening my heart to this little animal has helped me to open my heart in a lot of other ways, as well. And I have been fascinated to observe that the other dog lovers, whom I wind up talking to because of him, are the nicest people in the world.

FOR THE LOVE OF DOG

We Red Hatters love our pets so much that we sometimes even include them in Red Hat Society activities. Queen Charlotte Beasley of the Southern Belles of Boca Raton, Florida, has a tiny black Chihuahua named Sir Barks-A-Lot, who rode in the seat of honor—the queen's lap—when the Southern Belles participated in a parade. The queen wore a royal light-up tiara, a purple ball gown, a feather boa, and red gloves, and she carried a red parasol and purple fan. Her chapterettes wore glow sticks on their red hats and blinking pins on their clothing. Sir Barks-A-Lot wore a tiny red-and-purple jester's hat trimmed with red pom-poms.

The Crimson Chicks of Clearwater/Palm Harbor, Florida, turned a new puppy into an excuse for a party. Sandi McKendree, the "Queen Mother Hen," tells us that the group, which does something different together every month, finished up one summer gathering at the apartment of member Vicky Jensen, who had just gotten a new Chihuahua puppy named Orey. Vicky was surprised and thrilled to find that they had secretly planned a puppy shower for her! Sandi says that tiny three-pound Orey got a lot of gifts bigger than he is.

 "Dogs are children in fur coats."
—*Anonymous*

Virginia Zeidman, queen of the Fine Feathered Friends in Indian Wells, California, tells us about a contest held at a fundraising dinner for Guide Dogs of the Desert, an organization that trains dogs for the blind and disabled. Red Hatter Sylvia Allen-Wyder dressed her little white poodle, Precious, in a red hat, a feather boa, a string of pearls, and a purple tutu, and then painted her toenails and put some red bows in her fur. Sylvia donned her own finest red and purple and competed for the Arf-Cademy Award. Sylvia and Precious came in second, but Virginia says that Sylvia will always be number one to them.

 "I wonder if other dogs think poodles are members of a weird religious cult."
—*Rita Rudner*

This past summer, "PrinSis Jane," "Lady Bug Debra," and I joined Queen Linda Nargie and some of her chapterettes from the Hat Pack in Santa Barbara, California, to march with our dogs in that city's yearly Big Dog Parade. This parade proved to be a little more difficult for us Red Hatters to star in than most venues. I mean, how do you compete with dozens of huge Great Pyrenees dogs in a drill team or little girls in grass hula skirts marching with their dogs (in matching hula skirts and leis of their own)? And, as if these entries alone weren't enough to upstage us, the parade's opening entry was a skateboarding bulldog that actually demonstrated his skateboarding skill—pushing the board and hopping back on it every few feet—for the entire parade route! If nothing else, this parade makes very apparent the tremendous bond between dogs and their people—Red Hatters or otherwise.

Some claim that people and their dogs sometimes look alike. That is certainly open to debate, but it is undeniably true that dogs may experience similar emotions as their people at times. Rosanne Morrow of the Scarlet O'Haras in Grosse Pointe, Michigan, wrote: "When my son comes home for the summer from college, things have to change around the house. My husband and I are getting used to being empty nesters for short periods of time, and we have come to enjoy this time alone. When our son comes home, we have to rein in our habits and our fun. But I didn't realize until the other day that our dogs feel the same way. One of our dogs, Angel, a forty-pound adopted mixed breed, sleeps on our son's bed when he is away. Angel walked into his room this week and saw the disorder that is now everywhere in that room since our son's return. My dog stood on the threshold of the door, shook her head as if to say, No room at the inn for me, and walked out. Dogs have feelings, too!"

Ann Willoughby of the Crane Redhatters in Orange, Florida, shared a memory of a dog her mother, Pauline, bought in the 1950s. Sir Flagg LaVaughn was a registered Boston terrier, whom Ann and her brother Sid loved to play with in their yard. When they moved to a more rural area, Flagg was allowed to run around the neighborhood. One day, after going to play in the woods, Flagg didn't return. Concerned, Pauline went to look for him. To her horror, she found him caught in a trap that had been set for rabbits, his leg mangled beyond repair.

When she got the dog to the vet, Pauline called her children and told them that his back leg couldn't be saved. Either he would lose it or he would have to be put to sleep. Ann and her brother were horrified at the idea of putting Flagg down, and they insisted that they'd rather have a three-legged Flagg than no Flagg at all. They made a pact that they would never let him know that he looked any different from the way he had before, and they stuck to it. Flagg soon perked up, and before long he was playing as if he didn't even realize he was missing a leg.

One day when they were in the yard playing, Sid was holding a ball up and Flagg was standing on his back leg to retrieve it. A car drove by and one of the passengers pointed out the window and exclaimed, "Hey, everybody, look at the one-legged dog!" Ann says, "We laughed so hard, we cried. Afterward, Flagg was known as the one-legged dog."

I'm pleased to report that some sweet dogs are out there doing good in the name (or at least the regalia) of the Red Hat Society. Mary Cooper, my husband's aunt and queen of the Crimson Chaos of Costa Mesa, California, wrote in to let me know that the Red Hat Society now has some Good Samaritan–like canine members! The husband of one of her members is a dialysis nurse at a local hospital. One day, while working in the intensive care unit, he saw three therapy dogs, two of them wearing red hats and purple capes or boas. The third dog wasn't dressed up at all. Their owner explained that the dogs were Red Hatters and were there to cheer up the patients, but the third dog was a male and was too macho to dress up.

The newest honorary Pink Hatter of the The Red Hats Are Coming! The Red Hats Are Coming! chapter in Eau Claire, Wisconsin, is a Seeing Eye dog named Garlyn. Member Katherine Schneider says, "We're all familiar with the statistics about the increasing risk of developing various illnesses and disabilities as we age, but the Red Hat spirit of enjoying life, having fun, and making friends is a powerful medicine for healing the isolation that often goes with illnesses and disabilities." She says that their chapter is comprised of many who know that "it's the spirit, not the perfect health status, that matters in the world of Red Hatters." Red hats off to Katherine for saying it so well.

Peggy Ann Tuttle wrote in to say that her miniature white poodle, Cheyenne, helped her grandson Shane get over his fear of dogs—and Shane helped Cheyenne embrace the Red Hat Society colors! Peggy, queen mother of the Red Hats of Happy Rock, Gladstone, Oregon, left Cheyenne with her grandchildren for a few minutes while they were happily coloring. Even though Shane was deathly afraid of dogs, she figured it would be okay if she left the room for a little bit, since her other grandchild was with him (and since Cheyenne was lying quietly in the corner). When she came back, Cheyenne had been transformed from a fluffy white poodle into a red-and-purple hair ball! Shane and Lindsay, using red and purple crayons, had completely covered the dog's coat, including his tummy. It took almost four months for the color to grow out.

Merry E. Vargo of the Amies en Rouge in Bridgeport, Ohio, told me a BRH (before

Red Hatters) story about an elderly woman she met in line at the local fish and chips shop. Merry was there, grudgingly, because her husband wanted fish for supper, and she wasn't in the mood to cook. The other woman in line, a widow, was there to buy her dog his favorite meal. The food wasn't good for him, she explained, but that didn't matter, as she had to put him to sleep the next day, due to advanced cancer, and she wanted him to enjoy a last favorite meal.

Merry asked her if she would get another dog, and the woman commented that she feared she was too old to start all over with another puppy.

"Why don't you go to the shelter and get an older dog who needs a home?" suggested Merry. "They have a hard time placing them, so you'd be a genuine lifesaver for the dog."

"What do you mean?" asked the woman. Merry told her that if dogs weren't adopted within a certain amount of time, they were put to sleep. After paying for her dog's last meal, the woman turned to Merry.

"God must have sent you here," she said. "I was feeling so awful about the whole thing when I walked in. I feel so much better having talked about it. I think I'll be able to sleep tonight after all. Thank you so much for being here."

Since animals are always so ready to be there in the time of need for us, how could we do any less for them? Rebecca Hellams of the Mountain Divas in Lynch, Kentucky, found two tiny puppies on the steps of the community college where she teaches. Despite a horrific allergy to animal dander, she took the puppies home and tucked them onto the porch while she went to buy some puppy food for them and an antihistamine for herself. When she got back, she put on her slippers and went to check on the puppies on the porch, then tracked through the living room, looking for something for them to play with.

Poor Rebecca! Lacking experience with puppies, she hadn't realized that while what puppies do best is look adorable, what they do second best is . . . poop on the floor. Poop on the porch had led to poop on the slippers, which had led to poop on the living room floor. Rebecca dived for the carpet cleaner and tossed her slippers back out on the porch. She sprayed the cleaner on the carpet, walked into the kitchen with bare, slippery feet, and promptly fell on her face! She says, "Smack! Facedown, full body, kitchen floor, heavyset woman—SMACK! Additional side effects: husband laughing his head off. It took me a week to find homes for the puppies. I had pictures. I had the warm glow that comes from helping a helpless little bitty creature. I had a sinus infection and some less-than-impressive bruises. When you hit that hard, there should be more to show for it." I think God has a special place in heaven for people like Rebecca.

It is a shame, but allergies prevent many people from keeping their pets. Sandy Kangas, a member of Red Hatters of the North in Menominee, Michigan, took in a dog that was a few hours from being sent to the pound, purely because the owner's child was allergic to him. Sandy had recently mentioned to someone she knew that she'd love to receive a dog as a Christmas present, but her family had agreed long ago, before their Brittany spaniel died, that there would be no more pets for them. The next day, the acquaintance called to tell Sandy about this dog that was headed for the pound. Ed was a five-year-old "less-than-beautiful" mutt who was part hound. Sandy convinced her husband, Mike, to let the dog into their home, and he agreed, as long as Ed remained completely her responsibility.

"Guess who Ed bonded with?" writes Sandy. "Certainly not the one who saved him from the pound! It seemed the dog instinctively knew he had to win over Mike, my husband, in order to become a part of our household. He slept behind Mike's rocker, timidly cowered before him for a pat on the head, nudged his hand when it was time to be put outside, and on and on. The dog totally ignored me. This one-sided behavior continued for almost a year, during which time Ed never barked once, a rarity for a dog with even a particle of hound blood.

"Eventually assured that he had won his way into my hubby's heart, Ed decided he could finally begin sharing his time with me. The dog I had really yearned for finally became a part of my life, and it is wonderful, because he has a personality unlike that of any other animal I've known. Confident in our mutual love for him, Ed now bestows his royal blessings equally on Mike and me. On the downside, once he was totally comfortable in our environment, he began to bark. And bark. And bark. He is, as I said, half hound."

When our beloved dogs are gone, we mourn for them, sometimes terribly. Queen Ella Whitaker of the L.O.V.E. Red Hats, Middleburg, Florida, shared memories of her little "black curly-haired ball of energy," Nikki. Nikki's exuberant nature caused her to be terribly hard on their lawn, as she loved to pursue critters by digging for them, particularly moles. The yard really took a beating during the years Nikki was in residence. When Nikki became desperately ill, Ella spared no expense trying to keep her alive. But it was no use; eventually, Ella was forced, out of love for the dog, to have her put down. They took the little body home and laid it to rest in an area of their garden beneath a plaque reading NIKKI'S GARDEN. Ella says she will never again have to say, "Nikki, get out of the garden." But that is no consolation.

RED CAT SOCIETY

Cats are, if you will excuse the phrase, a whole different animal. Having had more cats than dogs over the years, I used to think of myself as a "cat person," whatever that is. (I still consider myself a cat person, but now I am also a dog person.) I liked their independence and self-reliance. I still believe they are among the most beautiful of animals, with their graceful movements, incredible eyes, and gorgeous variations in coat color and texture. Some of them live up to the general reputation that cats have: They are aloof and distant with their owners. Others apparently have not received word that they are not dogs: They purr and pester us for attention constantly. We have two cats, both black Siamese, one of which adores my husband beyond belief. Whenever he is home, she is either in his lap or draped across his shoulder, purring like a buzz saw. Me, on the other hand, she could do rather well without. The second cat seems to be lukewarm about both of us. She is, after all, a cat. But we can't help loving our cats, too.

As already noted, the Crimson Chicks

threw a puppy shower. But then, their member at least *had* a puppy. The Ya Ya Red Hats in Summerfield, Florida, threw a kitten shower for Queen Barbara LaVeille—complete with an adorable Siamese kitten to go with the gifts! When the animal is one of the shower gifts, I doubt that getting away with a surprise proves to be much of a problem. Fortunately, the queen says that she and her husband are thrilled with their new family member.

Have you ever heard of Take Your Cat to Work Day? One Halloween, Jane Barrett of the Seacoast Red Hat Mamas in Portsmouth, New Hampshire, needed a costume to wear to the Hallmark store where she worked. So she piled on every item of Red Hat Society regalia she had, including purple gloves and a red hat awash in purple and red flowers. She dressed her Himalayan cat, Sugar, in similar Red Hat attire and carried him along. Yes, *him*. Sugar is a boy. But he looked so ravishing in his hat and Boa that Jane couldn't resist putting a photo of him dressed up in his finest on her Christmas card a few weeks later. I don't know if Jane noticed, but, to me, Sugar looks a little annoyed in that picture.

HAVE CAT (AND POODLE) WILL TRAVEL

Red Hatters not only take their pets to work or on parade; they take them on vacation, too. Jean H. Coe of the Undecideds in Newton, North Carolina, found herself staring out the window at a motor home she had never driven, suddenly alone for the first time in her life. But one day, she realized she was not truly alone. She had her four-pound toy poodle, Killer, for company, and also a recently adopted stray kitty. Jean named the cat Genesis to symbolize her new beginning, and she was pleased to see genuine geniality develop between Killer and Genny. She quieted the voice inside— which was reminding her of an article she had read, warning that traveling with a cat in a vehicle could be torturous—and prepared a pet carrier with a fuzzy pink blanket. She was not prepared, however, for the cat's incessant meowing and the dog's accompanying barking. The only solution, according to Jean, was to put the cat in the back of the motor home and turn the volume on the tape deck up another notch.

Tisa Bell is queen of the Laughing Red (&

Pink) Hat Society in Encinitas, California. She planned to attend the San Diego Cat Fanciers Association Show and posted an invitation on our Web site for all local Red Hatters to join her there. What do you want to bet that she had a great time coming up with the wording for this invitation: "You'll flip as the flurry of fascinatingly fun festivities fill the fabulous facility and our flock of fashionably frocked female feline fanciers flaunting flashy fedoras fill the floor of the show hall to watch as the fancy, fluffy, frisky, flea-free felines frolic for feather and face the fair but finicky faculty of judges, and a few fortunate flawlessly fantastic feline finalists fetch fittingly favorable fanfare, flattery, and fame at the finish, causing felicity to be felt by the firm fellowship of female friends embracing folly." Tisa dares us to say this three times really fast!

Caren Belbey of the Hippie Hatters in Noblesville, Indiana, wrote to let us know about fellow member Elizabeth Rodeghiero, the "Princess of Prose," who keeps chapter members up-to-date on events. Elizabeth has a special cat sense: Each memo includes something about or from her cats. She came across a poem about cats (author unknown), changed a few words to her purpose, and sent it out to her chapterettes.

When I am an old cat
I shall wear a red diamond collar
And leave my footprints on white
*   couches.*
I shall drink cream with a touch of
*   brandy*
And spit out my vitamins.
I shall sit on the laps of dog people
*   (heehee)*
Just to irritate them.
I shall nap on the top of the neighbor's
*   petunias*
And perch on top of birdbaths and
*   grow charmingly chubby.*
But for now I must tolerate the dog
And use my litter box
And not sharpen my claws on the sofa
So no one can doubt the truth that
*   cats are superior to dogs.*
But every once in awhile I wonder
If I should be naughty now and then
*   and nip a few toes*
So my humans won't be too shocked
*   when suddenly*

*I become an old cat
And start to wear a red diamond collar.*

ANIMALS GREAT AND SMALL

Red Hatters enjoy adopting nontraditional animals into their families as well. Queen Linda Glenn, of the Rowdy Red Hat Mamas of Northwest Wisconsin (in the town of Luck), rescued a newborn white-tailed deer when the fawn's mother was hit and killed by a car in June of 2002. They bottle-fed her four times a day with lamb's milk replacer, and when they were certain that she was going to survive they named her Gabriella.

She lived outside in the grandchildren's play yard on their forty-acre farm. When she was about six months old they turned her loose to roam freely, but she refused to leave them. Obviously, in her mind at least, she was already home.

"Gabby" stays close to home, roaming pastures and forest. She hangs out at the farm with her friends, the dogs, cats, ducks, and horses. When invited to do so, she goes right into the house to visit and receive treats.

Linda says, "Gabby comes when called. Because she was raised around humans and domestic animals she is not totally nocturnal, as are most deer." Gabby attends multigenerational tea parties, plays tag with grandchildren, and enjoys the status of official member of Linda's chapter. Although she cannot attend most of their events, because she cannot ride in the minivan, she never misses a gathering at Linda's house. Gabby is very slender and graceful and she looks elegant in her red hat and boa.

She delivered her first fawn in May 2004, right in the farm's backyard. She and her son, Jack, continue to roam freely, returning to the house every morning and evening to visit "their" humans and enjoy treats.

On the other side of the pet spectrum is Daffy the Duck. Daffy began life as Daphne, until Pat Powers, who lives in Owasso, Oklahoma, realized that her duckling's head was turning the deep green of a male mallard. Daffy was raised with three dogs, and according to Pat, Daffy also thought that he was a dog. When the dogs ran up and down the fence barking at people, Daffy followed, making a beeping noise (apparently the closest he could come to barking). He also learned to whistle, having figured out that when he did that, their Lab, Sam, would come running. Ducks imprint on the first creatures they see, and Daffy, having learned to be a dog, couldn't fly. When the family tried to teach him to swim in a wading pool, at the beginning he could only paddle backward. Although he finally learned to swim, he never did quack; he only beeped.

The animals that touch our hearts are not always pets. All the creatures that live in this world deserve our respect. Dottie Winkelmann spent days keeping an eye on a robin's nest in her front yard. "I felt honored to have nature so close," she said. Dottie, a member of the Red Hat Honeys of the Fond du Lac Senior Center in Wisconsin, began leaving out bird food for the mother and was fascinated and touched by the way the little mother tended to her eggs. One night, during a thunderstorm, Dottie rushed outside to check on the nest, but it was gone! The mother bird sat there on a branch, looking forlorn. Dottie and her husband, Pete, got a flashlight and went searching for the nest and eggs. They found all three eggs a few feet away from the tree, lying on the ground. Pete secured the nest to the branch with string and they gently replaced the eggs in it. Dottie wrote, "We found one cracked egg on the sidewalk a few days later, but two of the baby birds survived that storm. In times of need, mothers can be there for one another. So can Red Hatters."

I have heard so many people say that once the children have gone and the last pet has died, they do not plan to replace the pet. When children go, they leave a huge empty space behind, but a good parent is happy to see them begin to build independent lives. This is the way it should be. When a pet goes, the hole it leaves behind does not have to be permanent; there are always plenty of animals that need homes. It is hard for me to understand why so many people deprive themselves of the love and companionship that a new pet can bring into a home with it when it moves in. No, animals do not take the place of children, but there is nothing like the solid warmth of a cat on your lap or the eager greeting of your dog at the door when you return home.

As long as you are a functional, involved person, caring for a companion pet can add a huge amount of joy to your life. . . . Go on—get another one!

10

Sharing the Good Stuff

I find television very educating. Every time somebody turns on the set I go into the other room and read a book.

—Groucho Marx

When I am attacked by gloomy thoughts, nothing helps me so much as turning to my books. They quickly absorb me and banish the clouds from my mind.

—Michel de Montaigne

Never judge a book by its movie.

—J. W. Eagan

Over the course of years, the methods we choose of entertaining ourselves will add laugh or cry lines to our faces, won't they? We may cry at sad movies and laugh at funny stories, but whatever our responses, they contribute to the texture of our experiences.

"You are what you eat," it is said. (Our resident humorist, "Dr. Maxine Harper," says that if that is true, she is cheap, fast, and easy. But that's another story.)

If the food that we eat literally becomes *part* of our bodies, isn't it fair to say that the thoughts and ideas we open our minds to literally become part of our minds—and, eventually, our spirits? If food with poor nutritional value harms our physical health, then the types of books, movies, and ideas we devote our attention to could logically be said to have detrimental affects on our mental and spiritual health. Or perhaps it is not so much that stuff like this will hurt us, but the fact that it won't do us any good. Even if certain material is not bad enough to be actually harmful, I contend that it might not be worth our valuable time.

Have you ever had the experience of spending a significant period of time trying to get into a new book? Sometimes you may read twenty, thirty, or more pages and find yourself unmoved and unengaged—even bored or on the verge of irritation. I used to think that if I had already devoted a significant amount of time to a book, I was somehow obligated to finish it before I could go on to something I might like better. In a way, I suppose, it was akin to the idea of finishing one's vegetables before having dessert. (Obviously just one more rule!) Wherever the attitude came from, it definitely had a grip on me. From time to time, the same sort of thing happened at the movies. I would sit through an entire two-hour film, even though I had started yawning in the first half hour. Heaven forbid that I walk out before I got my money's worth! This was before I realized that my *time* was my greatest treasure.

No more. As I get older and become more conscious of the value of time, and more aware of having less of it left, I am more determined to spend it wisely. If I start a book that is, in my opinion, poorly written, or full of characters I don't like or have no interest in, I simply close it and go on to something else. If I am sitting in a movie theater or (more likely these days) watching a DVD at home and find that I am not enjoying the experience, or at least learning something new, I don't finish watching the film. There are just so many worthwhile, interesting things to do that I am not willing to squander my precious time and attention on anything that I don't find enjoyable or edifying. I am willing to bet that most of you feel the same way.

Now, I don't meant to suggest that everything we read, see, or listen to has to be full of lofty ideas or concepts that necessarily have enormous value, but I am suggesting that this material should in some way *add* something to your life. It should be enjoyable, pleasant, thought-provoking—not just something barely adequate, something that you do to pass the time. Sometimes the best thing you can do for yourself is to see a hilarious movie or read a novel that stimulates you to give serious thought to a subject you haven't considered before. Sometimes the most healing or pleasurable thing you can do is lose yourself in a mystery or a historical novel. But you should *really like it*!

Since there are more books and movies available than any one person could ever possibly absorb, we don't want to waste our valuable time on the stuff that's not up to par. Wouldn't it be great if we Red Hatters could help one another go straight to the good stuff? That way, we could avoid all those half-finished books and half-viewed movies. Those of us who regularly visit the Red Hat Society Web site (www.redhatsociety.com) have been sharing recommendations on reading and viewing material for several years already. This has led to lively discussions and has expanded the enjoyment of books and movies for a lot of women. Sharing is a huge component of the Red Hat Society. We share experiences, good and bad, adventures, and opinions with one another.

Over the years, hundreds and hundreds of recommendations have been shared. On the following pages, you will find a list of recommendations sent by Red Hatters specifically for inclusion in this book. Some are already known and beloved classics; others are new, maybe even obscure. In most cases, only one book by a given author is mentioned, but I'd be willing to bet that if you like one book by a particular author, you will be interested in checking out his or her other books. Remember that our tastes vary somewhat. But I will wager that a lot of this material is well worth your time.

No, we don't always agree on everything. I am also not suggesting that everyone has identical taste. We all know better than that. There will be varying responses to similar material among us Red Hatters. But I am quite confident that most of our recommendations are well worth following up on.

BOOKS

Albom, Mitch, *The Five People You Meet in Heaven*

Allende, Isabel, *Daughter of Fortune*

Anderson, Joan, *A Year by the Sea: Thoughts of an Unfinished Woman*

Asimov, Isaac, *The Robots of Dawn*

Austen, Jane, *Pride and Prejudice; Emma*

Bach, Richard, *One*

Baldacci, David, *The Winner*

Bear, Greg, *Foundation and Chaos*

Berg, Elizabeth, *Never Change*

Binchy, Maeve, *Tara Road*

Bode, Eva, *When Roses Bloom*

Bolton, Martha, *Didn't My Skin Used to Fit?*

Bombeck, Erma, *Motherhood: The Second Oldest Profession*

Bova, Ben, *Voyagers*

Breathnach, Sarah Ban, *Simple Abundance: A Daybook of Comfort and Joy*

Brontë, Charlotte, *Jane Eyre*

Brown, Dan, *The Da Vinci Code; Angels and Demons*

Buck, Pearl, *Showboat*

Bujold, Lois McMaster, *Paladin of Souls*

Burns, Olive Ann, *Cold Sassy Tree*

Bush, Barbara, *Reflections*

Caldwell, Taylor, *The Testimony of Two Men*

Chang, Jung, *Wild Swans*

Chevalier, Tracy, *Girl with a Pearl Earring*

Childs, Laura, any of the books in the series Tea Shop Mystery

Collins, Gail, *America's Women*

Collins, Larry, *Falling from Grace*

Conroy, Pat, *The Prince of Tides*

Dallas, Sandra, *The Diary of Mattie Spenser; The Persian Pickle Club*

Defede, Jim, *The Day the World Came to Town*

DeMille, Nelson, *The Lion's Game*

Diamant, Anita, *The Red Tent*

Doig, Ivan, *Dancing at the Rascal Fair*

Drury, Allen, *Preserve and Protect*

Dunne, Dominick, *An Inconvenient Woman*

Erdrich, Louise, *The Last Report on the Miracles at Little No Horse*

Evanovich, Janet, *One for the Money*

Fielding, Joy, *Kiss Mommy Goodbye*

Fitzhugh, Louise, *Harriet the Spy*

Flagg, Fannie, *Fried Green Tomatoes at the Whistle Stop Café*

Frank, Dorothea Benton, *Sullivan's Island: A Lowcountry Tale*

Frey, Stephen, *The Day Trader*

Gabaldon, Diana, *Outlander*

Gaffney, Patricia, *The Saving Graces*

George, Elizabeth, *A Suitable Vengeance*

Graham, Winston, *Ross Poldark*

Graves, Robert, *I, Claudius*

Gregory, Philippa, *The Other Boleyn Girl*

Grisham, John, *A Painted House*

Guterson, David, *Snow Falling on Cedars*

Haddon, Mark, *The Curious Incident of the Dog in the Night-Time*

Haley, Elizabeth Forsythe, *A Woman of Independent Means*

Hartwick, Cynthia, *Ladies with Options*

Herbert, Frank, *Dune*

Hickam, Homer, *October Sky*

Hillenbrand, Laura, *Seabiscuit*

Hillerman, Tony, *A Thief of Time*
Hinton, Lynne J, *Forever Friends*
Holmes, Marjorie, *Two from Galilee*
Hosseini, Khaled, *The Kite Flyer*
Howatch, Susan, *Wheel of Fortune*
Isaacs, Susan, *Compromising Positions*
Jaffe, Rona, *Five Women*
Johnston, Joan, *The Rivals*
Karon, Jan, any of the books in the series The Milford Years
Keillor, Garrison, *Lake Woebegone Days*
Kidd, Sue Monk, *The Secret Life of Bees*
King, Cassandra, *Making Waves*
King, Stephen, *The Stand*
Kingsolver, Barbara, *The Poisonwood Bible*
Krakauer, Jon, *Into Thin Air*
Kreidman, Ellen, *Light His Fire*
Kurson, Robert, *Shadow Divers*
Kurtz, Katherine, any books of the Deryni and Adept series
Lahiri, Jhumpa, *The Namesake*
Lee, Harper, *To Kill a Mockingbird*
Letts, Billie, *Where the Heart Is*
Levin, Ira, *The Boys from Brazil*
Levin, Meyer, *The Settlers*
Lindbergh, Anne Morrow, *Gifts from the Sea*

Littauer, Florence, *Silver Boxes*
Lott, Bret, *Jewel*
McCaffrey, Ann, *The Dragonriders of Pern*
McDermott, Alice, *Child of My Heart*
McMurtry, Larry, *Lonesome Dove; The Last Picture Show*
Medlicott, Joan, *The Ladies of Coventry Send Their Love*
Meyer, Anton, *The Last Convertible*
Michener, James, *The Source*
Min, Anchee, *Empress Orchid*
Morgan, Marlo, *Mutant Message Down Under*
Ogilvie, Elisabeth, the *Tide Trilogy*
Pearson, Diane, *The Summer of the Barshinskys*
Pilcher, Rosamunde, *The Shell Seekers*
Reichman, Judith, *I'm Too Young to Be Old*
Richter, Conrad, *The Awakening Land*
Roberts, Cokie, *Founding Mothers*
Roberts, Nora, *Birthright*
Ross, Ann B., *Miss Julia Meets Her Match*
Rule, Anne, *The Stranger Beside Me*
Santmyer, Helen Hooven, *". . . And Ladies of the Club"*
Saunders, Lawrence, *The Second Deadly Sin*

Sebold, Alice, *The Lovely Bones*
Shreve, Anita, *The Pilot's Wife*
Shriver, Maria, *Ten Things I Wish I Would Have Known Before I Went Out into the Real World*
Smith, Betty, *Joy in the Morning*
Sparks, Nicholas, *A Walk to Remember*
Stegner, Wallace, *Angle of Repose*
Steinbach, Alice, *Without Reservations*
Stone, Irving, *The Agony and the Ecstasy*
Styron, William, *The Confessions of Nat Turner*
Swift, Graham, *The Light of Day*
ten Boom, Corrie, *The Hiding Place*
Thayer, Nancy, *The Hot Flash Club*
Trigiani, Adriana, *Big Stone Gap*
Tutu, Desmond, *God Has a Dream*
Updike, John, *Rabbit Run* and other books in this series
Uris, Leon, *Mila 18*
Van Tighem, Patricia, *The Bear's Embrace: A True Story of Survival*
Vincent, Eleanor, *Swimming with Maya*
Viorst, Judith, *Forever Fifty; Suddenly Sixty and Other Shocks of Later Life*
Warren, Robert Penn, *A Place to Come To*
Watson, Larry, *Orchard*

Wells, Rebecca, *Divine Secrets of the Ya-Ya Sisterhood*
West, Michael Lee, *Crazy Ladies*
West, Stanley Gordon, *Until They Bring the Streetcars Back*
Wilkinson, Bruce, *The Dream Giver*

 "It is true that we have only one life to live; if we read, we can live as many more lives and as many kinds of lives as we wish."
—*S.I. Hayakawa*

MOVIES

If we listed every movie that each of us has ever liked, the list would be miles long. But here are a few of the favorites Red Hatters sent in response to a request for inclusion in this book:

Adam's Rib
The Adventures of Otis and Milo
The African Queen
An Affair to Remember

Arthur
As Good As It Gets
Beaches
The Big Chill
Big Fish
Boys Town

Bringing Up Baby
Broadcast News
Burnt by the Sun
Calendar Girls
Casablanca
Castaway
Chicago
Chocolat
Cinema Paradiso
Collateral
The Color Purple
Dances with Wolves
Dangerous Beauty
Dave
The Diary
Dirty Dancing
Divine Secrets of the Ya-Ya Sisterhood
Enchanted April
Fiddler on the Roof
Forbidden Planet
Forever Young
Girls Just Want to Have Fun
Gone With the Wind
Grease
The Great Gatsby
The Green Mile

Harry Potter series
Hope Floats
The Horse Whisperer
How to Make an American Quilt
I Am Sam
The Inn of the Sixth Happiness
It's a Wonderful Life
The King and I
King of Hearts
Little Women
The Lord of the Rings series
The Manchurian Candidate
Midnight in the Garden of Good and Evil
Monsieur Ibrahim
Moonstruck
Mr. Holland's Opus
Mrs. Doubtfire
Much Ado About Nothing
My Big Fat Greek Wedding

Now and Then
*An Officer and a
  Gentleman*
On Golden Pond
Ordinary People
Out of Africa
*Pirates of the
  Caribbean: The
  Curse of the Black
  Pearl*
*Planes, Trains &
  Automobiles*
Pretty Woman
Pride and Prejudice
The Quiet Man
Rabbit-Proof Fence
Raising Arizona
*Real Women Have
  Curves*
The Red Violin
Regarding Henry
*Remember the
  Titans*
Return to Me
Secondhand Lions
*Sense and
  Sensibility*

Shirley Valentine
Shrek and *Shrek 2*
Silverado
The Sixth Sense
*Something's Gotta
  Give*
Somewhere in Time
The Sound of Music
Spider-Man and
  Spider-Man 2
Star Wars
Steel Magnolias
*Sweet Home
  Alabama*
*Terms of
  Endearment*
The Thorn Birds
*Under the Tuscan
  Sun*
Vanity Fair
Waking Ned Devine
West Side Story
Whale Rider
What About Bob?
Where the Heart Is
The Wizard of Oz
Yentl

These lists are, by necessity, hugely abbreviated. But it probably wouldn't be possible to come up with an exhaustive list anyway. We offer here only the tip of the iceberg. However, these suggestions are included for an important reason. I've said it before and I will say it again (probably a million times before I'm through): Sharing with one another is such a good thing. These little gems might be enough to prove to all of us, all over again, how easy it is to brighten the day of another simply by passing good things on. Anytime that we can add a bit of value to the life of someone else, we have done something worthwhile.

Afterword

If a man insisted always on being serious and never allowed himself a bit of fun and relaxation, he would go mad or become unstable without knowing it.
—Herodotus (c. 485–425 B.C.)

Herodotus knew this about 2,500 years ago; so why does it take so many of us so long to get the truth of it through our heads? Rather than dwelling on that question, we Red Hatters are intent on just getting on with it, allowing ourselves the "bit of fun and relaxation" that the wise Herodotus advocated. We are deliberately packing our lives with experience and meaning, focusing on the good stuff and refusing to dwell on the not so good. So we will continue to schedule regular fun for our chapters. And we are bound and determined to do a *lot* of laughing.

THINGS TO REMEMBER

1. No one can ruin your day without *your* permission.
2. Most people will be about as happy as they decide to be.
3. Others can stop you temporarily from doing something you want to do, but only you can do it permanently.
4. Whatever you are willing to put up with is exactly what you will have.
5. Success stops when you do.
6. When your ship comes in, make sure you are willing to unload it.
7. You will never have it all together.
8. Life is a journey, not a destination. Enjoy the trip.
9. The biggest lie on the planet: "When I get what I want, I'll be happy."
10. The best way to escape your problem is to solve it.
11. Ultimately, takers lose and givers win.
12. Life's precious moments don't have value unless they are shared.

Laughter is crucial to successful Red Hatting. Here's a little test, submitted by red-hatted humorist Joanne Augustine, to help you determine the current health of your funny bone. No one will grade this test—except you!

WHAT IS YOUR LQ
(LAUGHTER QUOTIENT)?

Write the number that is most true for you:

1 = almost never
2 = seldom
3 = sometimes
4 = often
5 = always

_____ I hear myself laughing out loud.
_____ I am a fun person to be with.
_____ I play spontaneously.
_____ I feel okay about acting silly in appropriate situations.
_____ I regularly plan times for playing and laughter. (If you are a Red Hatter, the answer to this one has to be at least a 4.)
_____ I can laugh at my own mistakes.

_____ I make the best of bad situations.

_____ I use humor to make others feel better.

_____ I avoid using humor that makes others feel uncomfortable.

_____ I avoid sarcastic and negative humor.

_____ I can see something positive in most situations.

_____ I take time out for the holidays.

_____ My family and friends support my need for fun.

_____ When I feel stressed, my sense of humor keeps things in perspective.

_____ I feel comfortable laughing at work.

_____ I allow myself to play first and work later.

_____ My sense of humor is one of my best qualities.

_____ I believe laughing contributes to my sense of well-being.

_____ The more I laugh, the better I feel.

Put your total score here: _____

If you scored:

75–100, high LQ: You're doing fine. Keep it up.

50–75, average LQ: Pretty good, but it could be better.

25–50, low LQ: Look back over the questionnaire and see what you need to do to tickle your funny bone and get more laughter out of life.

There are neither rewards for a high score on this test nor penalties for a low one. But I hope you have received something beneficial from taking it—food for thought.

I am aware of no written test to measure how well each of us deals with the painful parts of life. Life itself provides that test, I suppose. It is a certainty that hard times will visit each of us, perhaps a great many hard times. We cannot avoid them; we can only deal with them in the same manner in which they befall us—one at a time. It seems to me that this laughter IQ test contains a few clues as to how to make the best of even the worst circumstances. Even when we are in great pain, it is helpful to study the situation and find *something* over which we can gain some control. In the midst of a loss or a defeat, perhaps we can find the strength to take a moment to feel gratitude for the good things that we have left in our lives. Perhaps we will find strength by spending extra time with those closest to us, by giving ourselves a break to visit a peaceful spot to pray, or even by remembering to take pleasure in the smallest of lovely moments. In any event, it is a given that our cry lines will bear testimony to the years we have lived, just as our laugh lines will.

Do yourself, and the rest of us, a huge favor: Come out to laugh if you can and cry when you must, but do it with the rest of us! Life is easier when it is shared with people who care about you. The Red Hat Society has its doors thrown wide open!

Appendix

Oh how we love our names!

In our first book, we listed some of the most creative titles and chapters. But just when we think that there are no clever names we haven't heard yet, more great chapter names keep getting registered.

Sometimes humor is only one attribute of these chapter names. The Oxytocin Chicklets are in Riverview, New Brunswick, Canada. Queen Mother Wendy Pooley reports that their name was inspired by biology—and by daytime television. "On his TV show, Dr. Phil said that when women gather together, their bodies produce a feel-good hormone called oxytocin. This hormone is essential for our mental and emotional well-being. When the Chicklets are together, the oxytocin is flowing and flowing and flowing!"

Queen Shirley Presson's chapter in Mc-Kinney, Texas, named itself the Ripe Tomatoes. Their younger members (Pink Hatters) are the Green Tomatoes.

How about these chapter names?
Pompous Sasses—Pace, Florida
Is It Hot or Is It Me?—Peoria, Florida
REDegades—Carthage, New York
Some Like It Hat—chosen by chapters in
   both Draper, Utah/and Dumfrees, Virginia
Out to Lunch Friday Bunch—Hampton,
   Virginia
Royal Pains—Palm City, Florida
Amazing Grapes—Casa Grande, Arizona,
   and Palm Coast, Florida
Endorphin Divas—Allen, Texas
Not So Prim Roses—Sneads Ferry, South
   Carolina
Love Life—Oakland, California
A Lot of Tickled Pinks and One Red
   Beauty—Brea, California
Red and Pink in Synch—O'Fallen, Illinois
Bee-You-Tea-Full Dreamers—Lititz,
   Pennsylvania
Strawberry Smoothies—Rochester, New
   York
Senior Moments—Fort Morgan, Colorado

Rust-Proof Red Hatters—Placerville, California

Little Red Rockers—Little Rock, Arkansas

Ravishing Relics—Table Rock, Nebraska

Happy Hour Hooligans—South Coast Metro, California

Washago Wonder Women—Washago, Ontario, Canada

Hatters Without a Cause—Lynchburg, Virginia

Queen Quahog and the Little Necks— Yarmouth Port, Massachusets

Sisters of Perpetual Whoopee— Minneapolis, Minnesota

I Wannas—Council Bluffs, Iowa

Tilted Chapeaux—Nokomis, Florida

Red Hat Rat-A-Tat-Tats—Boynton Beach, Florida

Traveling Tea Pots—Rochester Hills, Michigan

Wrinkle Queens—Two Harbors, Minnesota

Stark Ravin' Mad Hatters—Starke, Florida

The Heady Lamar Red Hats—Rochester, New York

Hopulikit Red Hat Society—Portal, Georgia

Tootie Frooties—Sheffield, Iowa

KA-Weenies—Long Beach, California

The No-Faults (Yes, We're Perfect)—San Bernardino, California

Nubian Bootscooters—Los Angeles, California

The High Tea-ers—Lansing, Michigan

D'HEC with 50—Lexington, South Carolina

The Bloomin' Cherries . . . Cuz We're Not Ripe Yet—Clarksville, Tennessee

Belleoma (Belle means beautiful and Oma means grandma)—Bellevue, Nebraska

Fine Red Whines—Mooresville, Indiana

De-Stressed Damsels—Oak Creek, Wisconsin

Giggling Grannies—Indianola, Nebraska

Hat Pin Honeys—Spring Grove, Pennsylvania

Sierra Tiaras—Pollock Pines, California

Good Measure Quilting Q-ties—Carnegie, Pennsylvania

That's Th-hat—Dennison, Illinois

Pinks for Now—Portage, Michigan

Sew Forgetful—Rochester Hills, Michigan

The Casual-Tees—San Dimas, California

Purple People Meeters—Syracuse, Utah

Over the Summit Red Hat Society—Tacoma, Washington

Silver Teapots—Penfield, New York

ReRuns—Brazoria, Texas

NuBee RuBees—New Bethlehem, Pennsylvania

Red Tails in the Sunset—Minneapolis, Minnesota

Tundra Tootsies—Eagle River, Alaska

Mascots R Us—Internet-only chapter for mascots

Red-U-Cators with Hattitudes—Simi Valley, California

Magenta Yentas—Parma, Ohio

Butt-E-Babes—Butte, Montana

Red-E, Set, Go!—Lemoore, California

Huffs and Puffs—Hogansville, Georgia

Red Hot Chocolatiers—Hershey, Pennsylvania

Maid-en America—Juneau, Alaska

Sew Many Friends—West Nyack, New York

Over-The-Pill Gang—Overland Park, Kansas

The Gabbigals—La Vern, California

Power Surgers—Sault Ste. Marie, Ontario, Canada

Burnt Out Bonnets—New Brighton, Minnesota

Red e Or Not—Minn, Minnesota

Gallivanting Grannies—Lowell, Indiana

The Do's and Docents—Warwick, Rhode Island

Cellulite Sisters—Crandon, Wisconsin

The Red Aunts—Bell, California

Pinky Dinks—Oklahoma City, Oklahoma

Pink Champagne—New Milford, Connecticut

Scrap Happy Red Hatters—Chillicothe, Ohio

Have Feathers, Will Fly—DFW Airport, Texas

Oy Vey Sisterhood—Mt. Laurel, New Jersey

Red She Sez—Hampstead, Maryland

The Red Hat Sew-ciety—Roswell, Georgia

Jurassic Coast Fossils—Lyme Regis, Dorset, England

The Harried Potters—Carleton Place, Ontario, Canada

Loose and Limber Lovely Ladies—Duluth, Minnesota

Rojo Revelers—Bolivar, Missouri

Shrivelling Violets—Ripon, Wisconsin

Retro Rubies—Rochester, New York

Cloche Encounters—Mentor, Ohio

Ruby Red Sippers—Flat Rock, Minnesota

Purple Posse—Port Huron, Minnesota

Twisted Sisters—Hancock, Iowa

Twinkies Pinkies and the South Shore Shufflers—Portage, Indiana

Bement "Bowled" and Beautiful—Bement, Illinois

Sew We Go—Myrtle Beach, South Carolina

Whirly Twirly Red Hat Girlies—Ocala, Florida

Zippity-Do Dolls—Salem, Missouri

Red Ripple Rockers—Campbell River, British Columbia, Canada

Rip-Roaring Reducators—Gainesville, Georgia

Sassy Survivors—A group for breast cancer survivors

'57 Classics—Davenport, Iowa

Vul-can Trekkie Troopers of the Red Hat Society—Vulcan, Alberta, Canada

HRT Hatters Ready for Trouble—Wallace, North Carolina

The Fabulous Fortune-Tellers with the Fuchsia Fedoras—Las Vegas, Nevada

Our Turn Now Red Hatters—Louisa, Kentucky

Walkie Talkies—Poway, California

Noble Order of the Valkyrie Systers of Grace—Wichita, Kansas

Up North—Haslett, Michigan

Bear-ly Ladies—Long Lake, New York

Reigning Violets—South Salem, New York

Chili Colorado (Red Chili)—Denver,
    Colorado

Gr8ful Gals—Vermilion, Ohio

No Hat Left Behind—Harrisburg,
    Pennsylvania

Flittin' Jennys—Warm Springs, Georgia

Goodtime Grannies of Atria—East
    Northport, New York

Happy Heifers with Hattitudes—Ozark,
    Alabama

Forget-Me-Lots—Upper Sandusky, Ohio